CHESS

An · Illustrated · History

RAYMOND KEENE

SIMON AND SCHUSTER
New York London Toronto
Sydney · Tokyo Singapore

HALF-TITLE Pen drawing of a chess player by Jan de Bray (1661).

TITLE-PAGE An early nineteenth-century Indian set. Note the role of the elephants and the unusual introduction of a camel piece, reflecting local military conditions.

CONTENTS A selection of queens. It was not until the fifteenth century that the queen was transformed at a stroke from a piece of no great strength to one of devastating ferocity.

Simon and Schuster
Simon & Schuster Building
Rockefeller Center
1230 Avenue of the Americas
New York, New York 10020

Copyright © 1990 by Phaidon Press Limited
Text copyright © 1990 by Raymond Keene
Designed by Simon Bell

First published in Great Britain in 1990
by Phaidon Press Limited, Musterlin House,
Jordan Hill Road, Oxford OX2 8DP

Typeset by Tradespools Ltd, Frome, Somerset
Color reproduction by Novacolour Ltd, Birmingham
Printed in Italy by G. Canale & Co. Turin

1   3   5   7   9   10   8   6   4   2

Library of Congress Cataloging in Publication Data

Keene, Raymond D.
    Chess: an illustrated history / Raymond Keene.
        p.   cm.
    Reprint. Originally published: Oxford [England]: Phaidon, 1990.
    Includes bibliographical references (p.126).
    ISBN 0–671–70814–7
    1. Chess—History.   I. Title.
GV1317.K44   1990
794.1'09–dc20   89–48570
                                                          CIP

To Teeny Duchamp and John Cage

ACKNOWLEDGEMENTS

I must here record my thanks to those, more erudite than I, whose knowledge and suggestions have greatly assisted me in the writing of this history. First of all, I must thank David Spanier, whose idea it it was; then Dr Irving Finkel, Deputy Keeper of Western Asiatic Antiquities at the British Museum, who told me all I know about pre-classical board games, and Dr Ricardo Calvo of Madrid, who first put forward the elegant formulation that chess is 'Greek thought expressed in Indian language.' Thanks also to Rod Large, who introduced me to the concept that the armies of Alexander of Macedon might have been responsible for spreading Greek board games throughout Asia Minor; to Grandmaster Lodewijk Prins of Amsterdam, who once gave me a long and fascinating lecture on the transition of the elephant to the bishop; to Vivian Davies, Keeper of Egyptian Antiquities at the British Museum, whose work on hieroglyphs was also so helpful in this respect; to Gareth Williams whose help and extraordinary generosity resulted in the book having such a rich variety of illustrations; to Sarah Coombs, who was diligent with the picture research; to my wife Annette, who typed most of the book and is a constant inspiration; and finally to Grandmaster Yuri Averbakh of Moscow.

It is essentially to Averbakh that I owe the theory of the meeting of Greek petteia with Indian dice games along Alexander's route of Hellenic colonization, producing the earliest form of chess. There are various explanations for the origins of chess, but to me Averbakh's solution seems the most intellectually satisfying. Implicit in this theory is the belief that the origins of the chess must go back well beyond the sixth century AD date traditionally ascribed, for it is inconceivable to me that such enormous expertise, as undoubtedly existed in Baghdad in the eighth century, could have been possible if chess had simply been in existence for two hundred years previously. For this good, practical reason, if for no other (and it is a reason underestimated or ignored by other commentators), Averbakh has come very close to the truth. I am proud to present and endorse his theory here—for the first time, I believe, in print outside the Soviet Union.

Raymond Keene OBE International Grandmaster
London 1990

CONTENTS

INTRODUCTION   8

1 BORN IN BATTLE: ORIGINS OF THE GAME   11
   Shatranj: The Moves of the Old Chess   20
   A Game of Shatranj   21

2 THE RENAISSANCE EXPLOSION   23
   The Moves of the New Chess   28
   A Greco Game   34
   The Openings of the New Chess   40

3 THE PROFESSIONALS   43
   A Philidor Game   45
   'The Immortal Game'   48
   Paul Morphy: The American Meteor   56

4 MODERN TOURNAMENTS **63**
Crossplay of the Strongest Tournaments ever Held 67
A Capablanca Game 72

5 SOVIET HEGEMONY – WESTERN CHALLENGE **87**
Chess in Art 98
Spassky v. Fischer 105
The Hypermodern Openings 108
Kasparov v. Karpov 112

6 COMPUTERS **115**
Man v. Machine 118

CHRONOLOGY **124**

BIBLIOGRAPHY **126**

INDEX **127**

INTRODUCTION

'I approve strongly of rational games ...
for they serve to perfect the art of thinking.'
(Leibnitz)

CHESS is one of the world's oldest games of war, sharing a similar antiquity to the Chinese encirclement game of go, and the Japanese game, shogi. Chess is generally said to have developed in the north of India at some period before 500 AD. The original pieces, far less mobile than their modern counterparts, represented units of the ancient Indian army, foot-soldiers, cavalry, armed chariots and, of course, elephants. The fighting troops were led on the chessboard, as in real life, by the king and his senior minister, the vizier (which became the queen in the modern game). From India, it is said, chess spread through central Asia, China, Persia and Europe. The game was popular in Constantinople in the eleventh century, and was recorded as a favourite pastime of Byzantine Emperor Alexius Comnenus.

Once the game had reached the West, the identity and design of the individual chess pieces was gradually modified to reflect the social milieu of feudal Europe. The king, of course, remained unchanged, while pawns still represented infantry. The elephant, the heavy cavalry of Indian arms, was, however, replaced by the bishop, reflecting the power of the Church in the medieval landscape. The elephant, in any case, was virtually unknown as an engine of war in the West, the most notable example, perhaps, being Livy's mention of Hannibal's use of the beasts against Rome during the second Punic War on the Italian mainland. The horse of the Indian game, as one might expect, became the knight, the universally recognized symbol of feudal chivalry. The old scythed chariot became the castle ('Turm' in German, 'torre' in Spanish, 'tour' in French, naturally signifying 'tower') though, in English the accepted term is 'rook'. This word harks back to the ancient Persian word ('rukh') for war chariot or perhaps to 'rocco', an Italian alternative for 'tower'. Finally, the vizier was transformed into the queen, a vital component of the medieval court.

Towards the close of the fifteenth century in Europe a sweeping change in the rules spontaneously occurred. The most important alteration in the rules was the emergence of the queen, from being the creepingly feeble companion to the old king, to a phoenix-like resurrection as the most powerful piece on the chessboard. If one adds to this the double move available to pawns on their first turn, the ability of the new bishop to sweep along entire diagonals and the right to castle the king into safety, one virtually has the modern version of chess that is played worldwide today in 130 separate countries around the globe. This is the version officially recognized by the international ruling body of chess, the World Chess Federation, FIDE (Fédération Internationale des Échecs) which embraces over five million individual members.

Until the twentieth century chess was often regarded as a game for the aristocratic, wealthy or leisured classes of society. But today, to a certain extent as a result of the impetus given to chess in the Soviet Union after the Revolution of 1917, chess exerts a much broader appeal. If FIDE has five million registered players, the number represents but the minute tip of competitors, topping a vastly greater mountain of ordinary enthusiasts and lovers of the game. Indeed, in the Soviet Union, chess is the national sport, more popular than football. As a result of massive state encouragement for the game, Soviet grandmasters have more or less dominated world chess since the 1940s, although their superiority is fast being challenged by England, now established as the second strongest chess nation in the world. The USA is also a challenger for high honours in global chess terms.

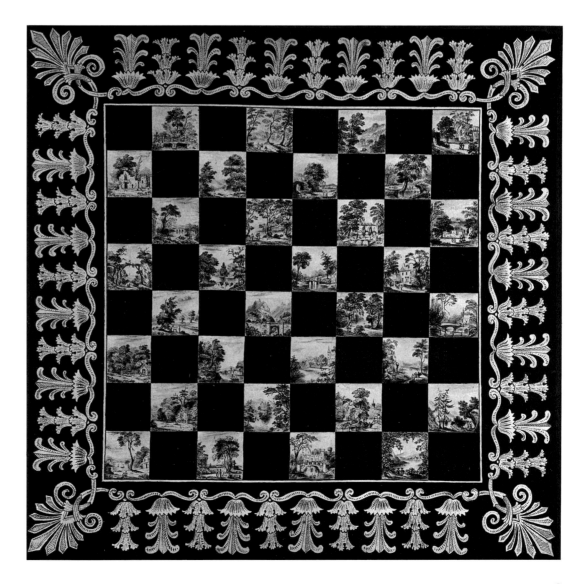

English pen and ink design for a chessboard, dating from the first half of the nineteenth century.

Amongst all the board games, chess appears to have the ideal blend of strategy, tactics and pure skill. Compare it, say, with backgammon, where the outcome is unduly influenced by the fortuitous throw of the dice, or with draughts, where the uniformity of the pieces tends to engineer a predominance of tactical solutions. The only games which compare in subtlety, science and depth with chess are shogi and go.

Chess is an almost perfect combination of art, investigative science, knowledge and inspiration. Analysing a game of chess is primarily an exercise in logic, yet executing a brilliant mating attack or solving a profound strategic question can also bring a genuine feeling of creative achievement. But chess is far from a solitary intellectual undertaking, like the solving of a crossword puzzle. The competition aspect of chess makes it a battle between two individuals, a battle without bloodshed, but still a fierce struggle of mind, will and, at the highest levels, physical endurance.

More than anything else though, chess has an ancient and distinguished history. The game provides a deep sense of continuity with the intellectual community of past ages, extending through hundreds of years and embracing all nations. In what follows in this book, the reader will discover positions devised a millennium ago, games played while the French Revolution was still a steely glint in Robespierre's eye, combinations calculated while the Kaiser was mobilizing his own pawns for the Great War. Such games still arouse admiration in those who play through them today. Perhaps in the future, readers of this book will find their own achievements adorning the literature of this fascinating production of the human mind.

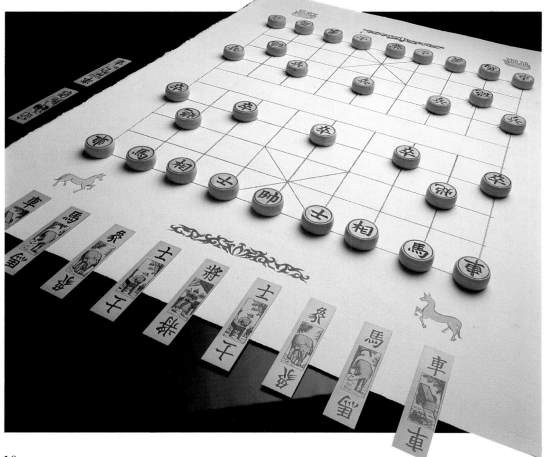

A Chinese chess set and board. The king sits in his fortress and a river divides the opposing armies.

10

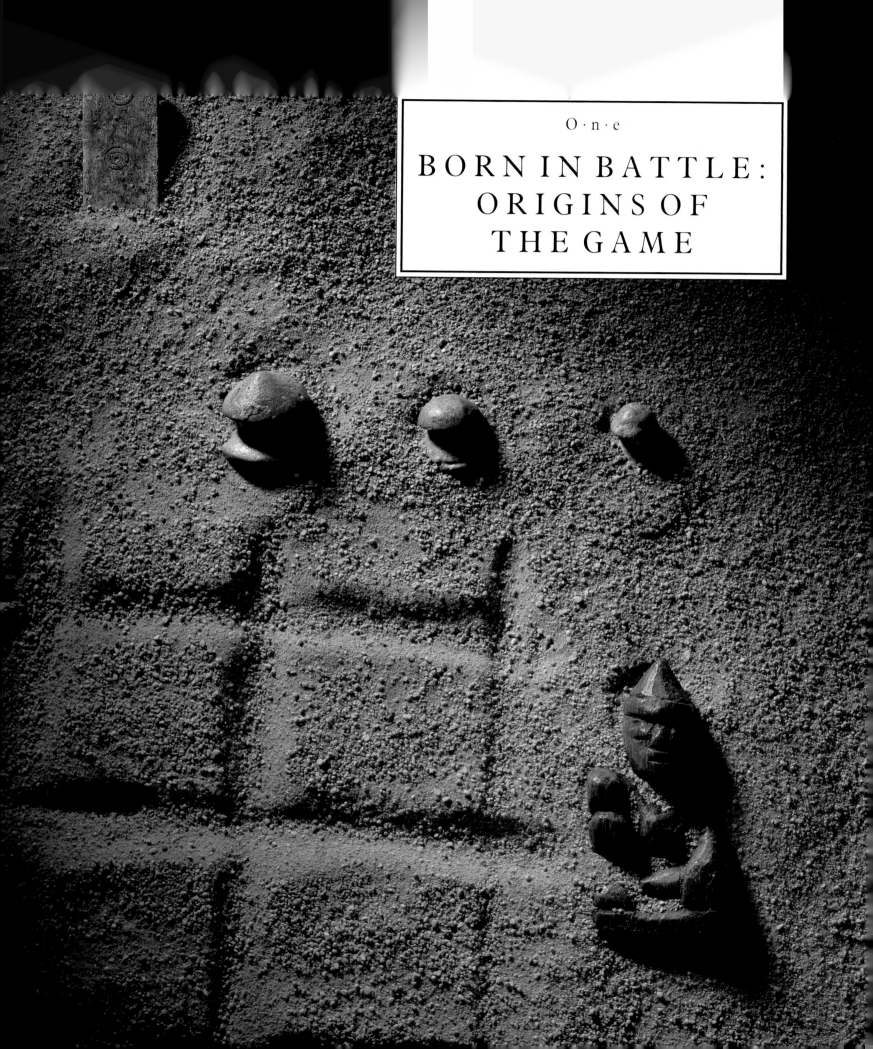

BORN IN BATTLE:
ORIGINS OF
THE GAME

CHESS, it is widely believed, originated as an oriental paradigm of battle around two thousand years ago. Various legends explain chess as a war game, starting in India, but it has also been theorized that the beginnings of chess can be found in the tactical battle plans of Alexander the Great from his Persian campaigns and beyond. Military formations, such as the Alexandrine phalanx and the parataxis, that of the later Byzantine Emperor Alexius Comnenus, were, it has been suggested, based on the number 64, the total of squares on the chessboard. In spite of its warlike origins, of whatever nature, chess remained, until the mid-fifteenth century, a game of slow strategic manoeuvre.

Man has probably sought relaxation through board games from the earliest times, and many different games must have come and gone, even before the emergence of chess itself. Archaeological finds from Egypt and Mesopotamia (essentially modern Iraq) provide the oldest evidence. The national game of ancient Egypt was senet, played on a board of 3×10 squares.

PRECEDING PAGE Pieces for a game played in sand: an early Roman piece (90 BC), a row of senet game pieces from 200 BC and an eighteenth-century Burmese king.

LEFT An Egyptian nobleman and his wife play at senet. Wall paintings such as this one were common, demonstrating that board games were an integral part of social life in ancient Egypt.

RIGHT A painting on an amphora made in Athens about 520 BC shows Ajax and Achilles playing a game that has often been described as chess but was more likely to have been petteia.

BELOW This is a question that has plagued chess historians more than any other. Here a contemporary advertiser offers his own solution.

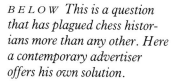

The origin of the ancient game of chess is the subject of a wellnigh hopeless controversy. By writers and in legends the distinction has been claimed for Egypt, China, India and Persia. Indeed, traces of the game extend to prehistoric times, and defy scientific investigation. The game was probably introduced into western Europe by the Arabs (circa 700). The term "checkmate" is derived from the Arabic al-shāh māt, meaning "the king is dead."

Senet typifies all known ancient board games in several important respects. It was a race game for two players, with competing sides controlled by dice, in the form of numbered cubes, throwsticks or knucklebones. While the players' skill no doubt had a part to play, this must always have been subsidiary to luck. Pieces might battle, and perhaps knock one another off the board. But the winner of the game was the first one home round a specific track, and there was no element of tactics, strategy or mastery of territory. Senet boards are known from before 3100 BC and the game lasted in Egypt down to about 350 AD. Many boards have been found in tombs, but the game is hardly known at all outside Egypt.

The 'Game of Twenty Squares', well known from the boards discovered at Ur by Sir Leonard Woolley, in contrast to senet, was played all over the ancient Near East. Boards have been found in Iraq, Iran, Egypt, Cyprus, Syria, Turkey, Lebanon and possibly even as far as the Indus Valley. They range in date over the third to the first millennia BC. This too was a race game for dice and pieces, and it is possible that the Indian game of pachisi and chausar (from which modern ludo is derived), grew out of a game of this type.

In ancient Egypt boards for this game and senet were often combined in elaborate games boxes. A satirical papyrus shows a goat playing a lion at one of the two games. A third game that also spread in the ancient Near East had a race track delineated by holes, in which animal-headed pegs were inserted, rather in the fashion of modern cribbage boards.

In broad terms the games of ancient Greece and Rome fall into the same category of dice-controlled race games. 'Ludus Duodecim Scriptorum' was played on three rows of 12 spaces, with three six-sided dice thrown through a dice-box. A simplified version in two rows, called 'Tabula', appeared during the first century AD, and is probably the direct ancestor of backgammon.

Such classical dice-based games were generically known as 'kubeia'. Nevertheless, an entirely different branch of Greek board games existed, collectively known as 'petteia'. These were games of a battle-type which demanded skill, logic and pure reason, not just the fortune associated with a throw of the dice. I will argue here, that the petteia form of game was the forerunner of chess.

The Greek writer Cratinus mentions petteia as early as the fifth century BC. References to it are widespread in classical Greek literature. For example, Plato (?427–?347BC) states quite clearly in *The Republic*, that petteia involves long training if skill is to be achieved. Plato, in addition, compares, in *The Republic*, Socrates' victims, who are finally cornered and made helpless by dialectic, to 'bad petteia players, who are finally cornered and made unable to move, by clever ones'.

Aristotle, at one time the tutor of Alexander the Great, writes in his *Politics* that, 'a citizen without a state may be compared to an isolated piece in a game of petteia.' All this sounds uncannily like a modern chess pedagogue discussing the necessity of proper training and the evils associated with getting an isolated pawn!

Petteia was a board game, or group of games, demanding pure reason, symbolizing warfare and played without dice. However, it was not yet chess. Around 330 BC, Alexander the Great invaded Persia and marched on towards Asia Minor and India. En route he founded Hellenic colonies which lasted for centuries. Many of these, by the way, were named Alexandria; the name still persists in corrupted versions: Kandahar in Afghanistan, Iskander near Tashkent. The Greek colonists, assuming they were good students of Plato and Aristotle, would have played petteia. Hellenic influence in this region would have been considerable!

The epic poem, the *Mahabharata*, is central to Indian culture. It is the longest poem ever written, extending for more than 100,000 stanzas, around 15 times the length of the Bible. The *Bhagavad Gita* is just a section of this vast poem. The *Mahabharata* even contains within itself a shorter version of the other great Sanskrit epic, the *Ramayana*. The *Mahabharata* goes back to the sixth century BC. Through this vast poem runs the ineluctable pressure of predestination in human affairs. Typically, human action is puppet-like, in the hands of the gods. Indeed, the Pandava prince in the *Mahabharata* loses his entire kingdom on the throw of dice. A culture which produced such an epic is liable to have as its predominant mode of board games, those which are determined by chance, by the throw of dice, rather than by the free will. A culture which believes essentially in free will, that human beings are in charge of their own affairs, will play a quite different type of game. These will be games where strategies are conceived totally by the players, without the intervention of the chance element of dice. This was precisely what characterized the Greek petteia.

Sure enough, chaturanga has been identified as just such a dice game, played in India during the long period when the *Mahabharata* (an epic of battle) was achieving its definitive form. Chaturanga is the earliest precursor of chess that has been clearly recognized. The Sanskrit name, meaning 'Divided into Four', was also a term for the Indian army of the time, which was composed of four divisions: the elephants, the chariots, the cavalry

The board for the 'Game of Twenty Squares', discovered at the third-millennium BC site of Ur by Sir Leonard Woolley. The richness of design indicates that the aristocracy enjoyed

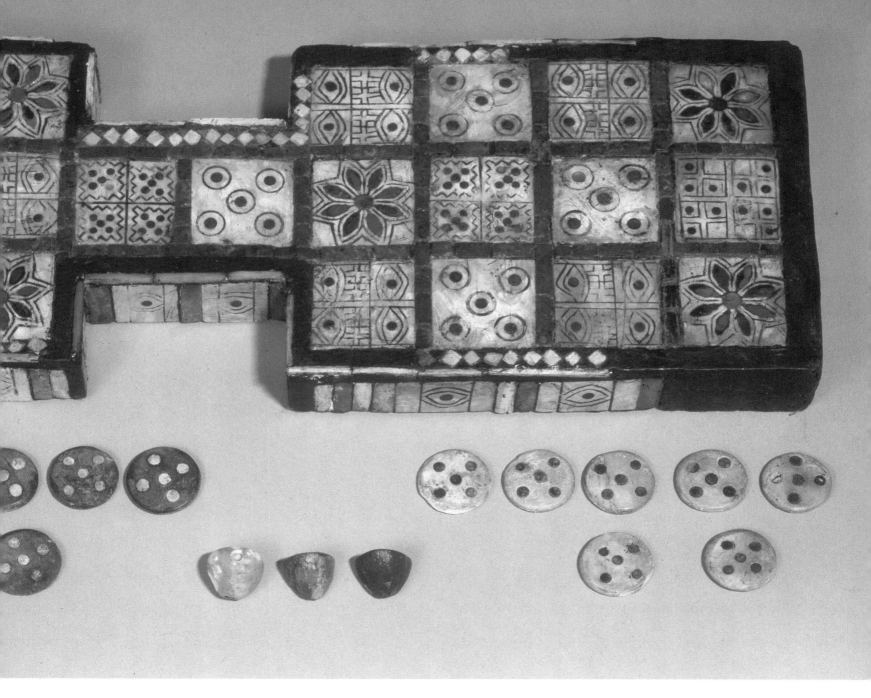

betting on stone horses when the racing season was over. Race games and games of chance predate games of skill and intellect such as chess.

and the infantry. The word 'chaturanga' may look alien, but it becomes less so if one thinks of the Latin, French, Spanish or Russian words for 'four'. Indeed, dwell on 'quarter angle' for a moment, and the linguistic roots in the Sanskrit become even more obvious. Documentary evidence for this dice game exists from the beginning of the seventh century AD. It is, however, more than likely that its ancestry is vastly more ancient. Indeed, it is my contention that in the centuries after the establishment of the Hellenic colonies on the route of Alexander, chaturanga, the Indian war game of chance met petteia, the Greek game of reason. From this meeting, from this concatenation of cultures, chess was born. The liberating effect of petteia was to eliminate the dice element from chaturanga.

15

Chess, for this is now what the game indisputably was, swept both east and west. By 800 AD, the Chinese already had their own version, where a central river divides the hostile forces; through Korea, the game reached Japan, where it is still played under the guise of shogi. In the Japanese version, captured pieces do not vanish permanently from the board, they go over to the enemy. Perhaps this indicated that Japanese battles of that period were fought with mercenary armies, which defected to the other side when defeat had become inevitable.

Chess moved west with even greater force. After the explosion of the Arabic expansion of the seventh century, the game, now known as shatranj, enjoyed a golden period. It reached Europe via the Moorish invaders of Spain, through the Byzantine empire and through Russia. However, it was during the eighth and ninth centuries in the caliphate of Baghdad of the Abbasid dynasty, that the game truly flourished. (Baghdad was, in fact, to shatranj, what Moscow is to the modern game.) Grandmasters developed, the subtlety of whose play (which still survives in brief published fragments) rivalled that even of modern masters. Among such were: Rabrab, Ar-Razi, Al-Adli, As-Suli and Al-Lajlaj ('The Stammerer'). The profound expertise of these players is evidence to me that shatranj was the product of an immensely long heritage. Such honed excellence does not burst forth unannounced in a new game after a mere century or so. Even with the improvement in means of travel, and hence communications, which was to take place in the post-medieval world, there was still to be a gap of three centuries between the advent of the Renaissance new chess and the arrival of a master such as Philidor. Yet the Baghdad caliphate could boast several players whose relative strength was comparable to that of the great Frenchman.

Designer chess pieces for the Middle Ages. These are known as the Charlemagne pieces, but they were not used by Charlemagne himself. The design however is so opulent that it is likely that they formed part of a royal collection.

Whalebone chess pieces found in Dorset, England, from the tenth or eleventh century, exhibit evidence of the Muslim influence on the respresentation of figures. The larger piece, though mainly abstract, has two small heads, apparently of horses. The small piece is a pawn.

The diagram below shows the development of the Egyptian hieroglyphic sign of the bull's head via Greek to the Latin letter 'A'. The ox, the most important component of primitive agricultural economy, naturally provides the basis for the first letter of the alphabet. It can be observed from the table how the horns of the ox have been gradually transmuted into the inverted crossed bars of the letter 'A'. The ox in Greek, 'aleph', the most vital animal, is also 'alpha', the beginning of the system of written symbols.

Egyptian	Protosinaitic	Phoenician	Early Greek	Greek	Latin
ᛦ	ᛘ	ᛣ	A	A	A

The elephant, apart from being the world's largest land-dwelling mammal, is also a chess piece. In the course of its long history it has undergone an interesting transformation from pachyderm to prelate. Alexander the Great and his troops encountered Indian war elephants on their campaigns, and the Greeks, seeing elephants for the first time, and observing their key role, in both oriental warfare and agriculture, named them 'aleph-hind', the 'Indian ox'. (The Spanish Conquistadores of the sixteenth century committed a similar error with llamas, calling them 'native sheep'.) The elephant, of course, appeared as a unit on the primitive Indian chessboard, the symbol of warfare in miniature.

Only in Russia and some Slav countries now, does the word 'elephant' ('slon') persist. Elsewhere, as chess progressed westward it was the 'l' 'f' sounds of 'aleph-hind' which survived. One sees traces of this in the Arabic term, *fil*; in the Middle English, *aufin*; in the Spanish, *alfil*; in the Italian, *alfiere*; in the German, *laufer*; Dutch, *loper*; the Serbo-Croatian, *lovac*; and perhaps even in the French, *le fou*.

It is evident that the various incarnations of the bishop in European culture have laid greater stress on preserving the ancient and original sound than the meaning. The Dutch and Germans see this diagonal piece as a 'runner'; the Yugoslavs as a 'hunter'; the French as a 'jester'; while the Spanish and Italian words, closest of all to 'aleph-hind', mean only the chess piece and nothing more. The English bishop is furthest, indeed, quite remote from its elephantine original. Nevertheless, when one construes a medieval court and its most powerful figures as the respective sides of a chessboard battle, then inclusion of the clergy makes perfect sense. More so, indeed, than jesters, runners, hunters and so on.

Table 1   Names of chess pieces

English	King	Queen	Rook	Bishop	Knight	Pawn	(Castling)
French	Roi	Dame	Tour	Fou	Cavalier	Pion	(Roque)
German	Konig	Dame	Turm	Laufer	Springer	Bauer	(Rochade)
Italian	Re	Donna	Torre	Alfiere	Cavallo	Pedone	(Arrocco)
Spanish	Rey	Dama	Torre	Alfil	Caballo	Peon	(Enroque)
Russian	Korol	Ferz	Ladya (boat)	Slon (elephant)	Kon	Peshka	(Rokirovka)
Arabic	Shah	Firz	Rukh	Fil	Faras	Baidaq	*(did not exist)*

English also has an exception in its word 'rook', where most European languages go for 'tower' or 'castle' (tour, Turm, torre). Doubtless, a key derivation here is from the alternative Italian word for tower, 'rocco'. In other European languages one sees the roots of 'rook' in the word for castling (roque, arrocco, enroque). The Russian for rook (boat)

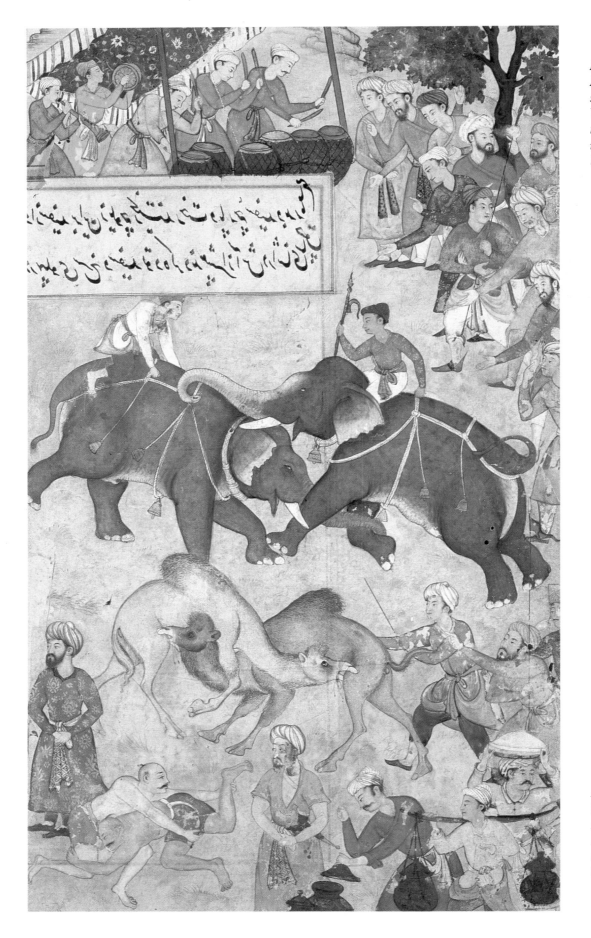

Elephants in combat from a Moghul miniature depicting a scene of royal sports at Agra. Who would have thought that these mighty beasts would have ultimately been reincarnated as bishops on a chessboard?

A nineteenth-century chess-board from Sind in western India, painted on wood. Perhaps the circular design is an echo of the round chess-boards of the Byzantine period.

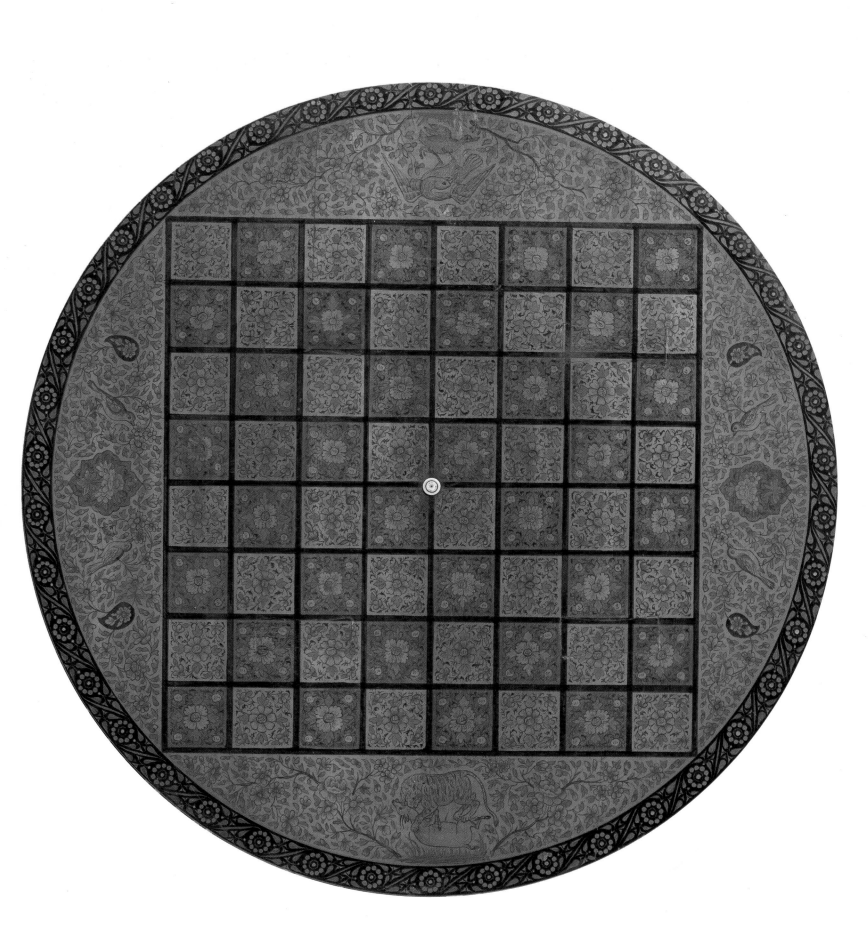

Shatranj: The Moves of the Old Chess

The *shah* (king) could move, as in modern chess, one square in each direction. It should be noted that stalemate, a draw nowadays, resulted in shatranj as a win for the player giving stalemate. It was also possible to win by baring the opposing king of all of its supporting pieces. Checkmate was not the only way to gain ultimate victory.

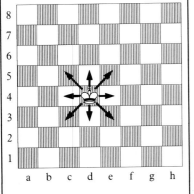

The *firz*, or *firzan* (vizier), was one of the weaker pieces on the board. It could only move one square diagonally in each direction. Of course, the feeble *firz* was to grow into the modern queen.

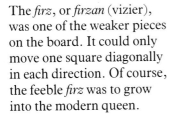

The *rukh* (rook) was the most powerful piece in Islamic chess. It moved in exactly the same way as its modern counterpart. However, castling was not possible as a speedy means of bringing the king into safety. Although I believe that the probable derivation of the word 'rook' in English is from the Italian 'rocco' (tower or castle) it should not be forgotten that an alternative derivation comes from the Sanskrit 'Ratha', a chariot, via the Persian and Arabic 'Rukh'.

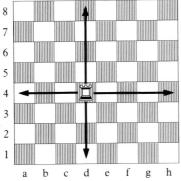

The *fil* (elephant/bishop etc.) was the weakest piece in Islamic chess. Although it could jump over other pieces, both friendly and hostile, its range was extremely limited. The diagrams show its powers and restrictions. From f1, the White *fil* could reach h3, d3, f5, b5, d7, h7 and b1. As can be seen, the White *fil* on f5 could leap over a White pawn on e6 to reach the d7 square.
The *fils*, unlike the modern bishop, do not cover b2, d2, e2 or g2.

The *fils* do not cover b6, b4, d6 or e4, g6 and g4.

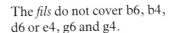

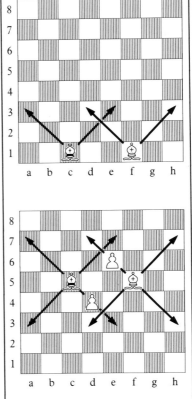

The *faras* (knight) was extremely powerful in shatranj, having exactly the same powers as the modern piece. It could leap over any

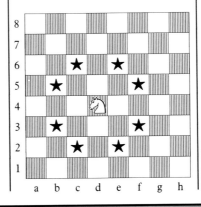

obstacle, and generally, in its surprise value, represented the cavalry arm of primitive fighting forces.

The *baidaq* (pawn), as in modern chess, moved forwards in straight lines but captured diagonally. The major differences from modern chess were the lack of the option of a double first move, the absence of the en passant option and the fact that the pawn could only promote to a *firz*. Pawns, of course, are foot-soldiers. One can still see the root in English 'pedestrian', for example. The words 'sepoy' and 'psahi', are both cognate military terms.

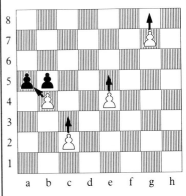

A Game of Shatranj

The following game by As-Suli was played in the tenth century in Baghdad. The game has been reconstructed from As-Suli's analysis by the international experts, Kenneth Whyld and David Hooper. An unknown weaker opponent plays White and the Grandmaster ('Aliya') As-Suli plays Black. In this game it is Black who makes the first move. Indeed, it should be observed, that even until the mid-nineteenth century, the convention did not exist whereby the player of the White pieces made the first move.

White: Unknown;
Black: As-Suli
Baghdad tenth Century AD.

1 ... f6   **2** f3 f5   **3** f4 Nf6
4 Nf3 c6   **5** e3 c5   **6** Flh3 g6
7 Nh4 e6   **8** b3 Fze7   **9** Fze2
Flh6   **10** g3 Kf7   **11** Nf3
Rd8   **12** Ne5+ Kg8   **13** Nd3
d6   **14** Nf2 Nc6   **15** d3 b6
16 e4 fxe4   **17** dxe4 d5
18 Fzd3 c4   **19** bxc4 dxc4
20 Fzxc4 Fla6   **21** Fzd3
Rac8
22 Nc3 Nb4   **23** Na4 Rxc2
24 Flf1 Flc4   **25** Nh3 Nxe4
26 a3 Re2+   **27** Kd1 Nxd3
28 Flxd3 Rxd3 checkmate.

An illumination in a medieval Spanish manuscript shows two Arabs playing shatranj. The game would have been played to exactly the same rules as those governing the game of As-Suli on this page. Note that the convention was to have the diagram sideways (from a modern point of view), depicting in two-dimensional terms exactly how the game was progressing.

Position after **10** ... Kf7.

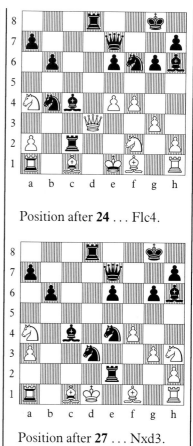

Position after **24** ... Flc4.

Position after **17** ... d5.

Position after **27** ... Nxd3.

The openings in Islamic chess were well documented. Some had romantic names, such as 'the Sword Opening', or 'Pharaoh's Fortress'. Others sound more eccentric to modern ears, for example, the 'Watad al-Fazz' ('Goat Peg') opening. Another strange one was the 'Ghariba wa Malubi' ('Wonderful and Lovely') opening. These set Arabic opening arrangements were called 'tabia'. The opening used by Black in the game above was a 'Mujannah' ('Flank') opening.

appears to be absolutely unique and has no connection with warfare. It is, indeed, amusing to see Russians referring to chess pieces, which evidently represent castles, as boats.

By the year 1000, chess was widely known and popular throughout Europe. Nevertheless, the great technical expertise and lust for knowledge of the Arabs was being gradually extinguished. With the decline of Baghdad, the writings, games and accumulated chess wisdom of As-Suli and his colleagues dispersed and vanished. For the following centuries, chess became, through the medium of tricky composed problems, part of the repertory of itinerant entertainers. Many of these, though, were ignorant of the strategy, tactics and even the rules, of the game itself. Still, the popularity of chess, at the common level, can be gauged, for example, from the Isle of Lewis chessmen. This was a cache of carved walrus ivory Scandinavian pieces dating from the twelfth century. The vast horde of disparate pieces, now in the British Museum, suggests that this was the stock of a merchant supplying chessmen to numerous clients.

During the medieval period, chess was mentioned in courtly tales and both Carolingian and Arthurian romances. A notable Arthurian reference can be found in the Welsh compilation, the *Mabinogion*. After a lengthy oral tradition, the stories which go to make up this national epic were finally written down in the thirteenth century. In the story of 'The Dream of Rhonabwy', King Arthur himself contests the battle boardgame 'Gwyddbwyll', against the Welsh hero, Owein. In the background fierce warfare rages between Arthur's pages and the black ravens of Owein. The symbolism argues that Arthur and Owein are playing chess.

In the Middle Ages chess, as symbolism, flourished, but as a science, as a serious game of reason and strategy, it was now running out of energy. The intellectual fire, the mental acquisitiveness of the great Arab practitioners, had been exhausted. As it was the Greeks who gave the initial impetus to chess, so it is to the Renaissance that we must look for the regeneration of the game.

Lancelot playing at chess on a magic board on which the pieces move of their own volition. He wins the game and is given the board, which he sends as a present to Queen Guinevere. The pieces are clearly visible on the board, which is of lapis lazuli bordered with gold. Chess in the Middle Ages was a potent symbol of stylized battle for the chivalric classes.

OPPOSITE French faience playing set, manufactured since the eighteenth century.

22

THE
RENAISSANCE
EXPLOSION

DURING the late fifteenth century the surprisingly rapid process had been initiated, whereby chess emerged from its slow, tortuous, medieval form. Suddenly castling was introduced, pawns gained the privilege of moving two squares forwards at their first turn, and the queen was transformed at a stroke from a waddling cripple (the Arabic vizier) to a unit of devastating ferocity. Perhaps the sudden access in strength of this piece helps to explain the joyous adventures and excursions with the queen which can be observed in the games of players of the new chess in the fifteenth, sixteenth and even early seventeenth centuries.

If chess is truly a symbolic game of warfare, then the increased firepower of the queen surely mirrors the contemporary introduction of artillery, as a long-range means of molesting the opposition, in the sphere of battlefield technology. These sudden developments

RIGHT French ivory mirror case of the fourteenth century. Courtly pursuits such as chess playing were appropriate motifs on luxury items produced for a sophisticated audience.

BELOW 'The Garden of Love' by Master E. S. (1440/ 50). Chess naturally took its place among activities here, being symbolic of complex relationships.

A knight from the Lewis chess set. The glum expression worn by all the pieces belies that fact that the twelfth-century walrus ivory carver from whose extensive stock they came must have been doing a roaring business, since a total of 67 pieces was found in his hoard at Uig in the Hebrides. The Lewis chessmen constitute the oldest complete set in existence.

A tenth-century ivory piece from Iraq. The elephant wakes up when placed on the chessboard!

The Moves of the New Chess

The *king*, as in shatranj, moves one square in any direction. Stalemate, the inability of one side to move at all, now results in a draw. I find this incredibly illogical, but there it is. It seems to me, that reducing your opponent to utter paralysis should be sufficient proof of victory, but modern rules dictate otherwise, and we must abide by them. Baring the king in modern chess by no means indicates victory (another illogicality?). In fact, the ending of two knights plus king against lone king is a theoretical draw. In spite of one side's evidently huge material advantage, the two knights simply cannot force checkmate. In modern chess there is, ultimately, only one way to win – checkmate – the irrevocable cornering of the enemy king; of course, an opponent, seeing his situation is hopeless, may concede or resign, before checkmate is delivered. (For castling, see the section on the rook.)

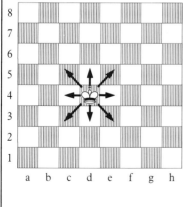

The *queen* is the most powerful piece in modern chess, and has been so since the middle of the fifteenth century. The diagram indicates her enormous range.

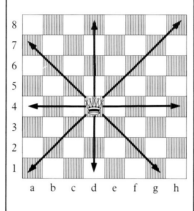

The *rook* moves as far as it can along straight lines, as in the Arabic game. Nevertheless, modern chess has introduced the castling rule. This is necessary, as modern pieces are so dangerous in comparison with their Islamic forebears, that there must be some method of swiftly bringing the king into safety. The

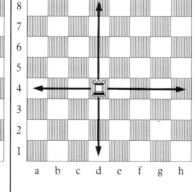

diagrams show the basic castling move, both king's side and queen's side, but also one key restriction: with

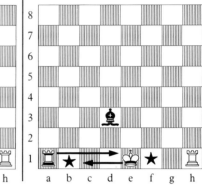

the Black bishop on d3 controlling the b1 and f1 squares, White can castle queen's side, but not king's.

Effempio 3 ô.

Modo di prendere al nemico una Torre, oue- ro la Regina. Come nel nº 29º à car. 43 e 44.

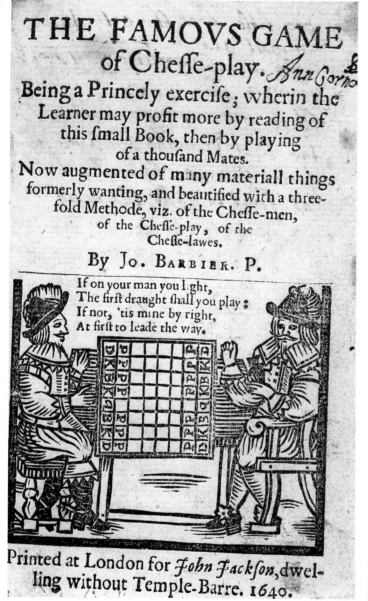

The *bishop* can no longer leap over obstacles, but it can now sweep along all the squares of its respective diagonals. A bishop, starting on f1, can reach, ultimately, every light square on the board.

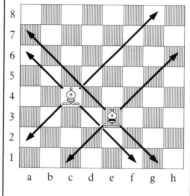

The *knight* moves exactly as in shatranj. The diagram shows its radius of action.

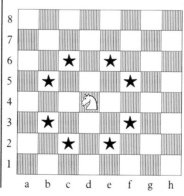

The *pawns* move exactly as in shatranj, except for the option of advancing two squares on the first turn and the ability to promote into any piece from a queen down. The second diagram shows the new en passant option, which could not have existed in shatranj: when a pawn exercises its double move, a hostile pawn on its own fifth rank, may still slip behind to capture it. Thus a White pawn moving in one go from d2 to d4, can be captured (on d3) by a Black pawn positioned either on c4 or e4. This rule is to prevent the game becoming too blocked and, therefore, drawish.

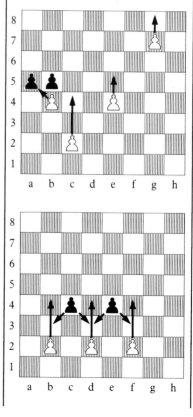

LEFT An illuminated page from a unique Italian manuscript entitled 'Il Dilettevole Givdizioso Givoco de Scacchi' (The Delightful and Judicious Game of Chess). The manuscript, dating from about 1730, is illustrated with 49 'examples' for the instruction of beginners.

ABOVE Barbier's book was a republication of a well-known chess manual in which the rules for the modern form of castling were made explicit. Although castling had been in use among the more expert players in France and England since around 1600, there was still some confusion to be resolved about the positions of the king and rook after the move.

LEFT An international selection of queens – some already anticipating the deep pleasures of victory!

RIGHT A wonderfully decorated elephant from a nineteenth-century Rajasthani set. The war elephant was also used to transport the barrels of cannon to the battle-front.

in the game must be explicable in terms of the overall Renaissance dynamic – the increasingly urgent perception of distance, space and perspective which distinguished that period of human intellectual development. Perspective in art, the telescope and the microscope were parallel developments, or soon to come. Siege artillery played a major role in battering down the walls of Constantinople in 1453. The advent of the new chess, with its devastating innovation of the queen move, had nothing to do with the example of powerful, warlike females, such as Joan of Arc or Elizabeth I, nor was it a question of boredom with the old style of the game, except in a very general sense.

It should not be forgotten that Columbus, having discovered the New World for Spain, presented this mighty conquest to the Catholic Rulers, Ferdinand and Isabella, in the Noble Tinell Hall on his return – the very hall where Gary Kasparov won the Barcelona World Cup of 1989! In 1519, Magellan set off down the Guadalquivir River in Seville, on the first circumnavigation of the globe. In 1987, Kasparov and Karpov contested in that same city, the first all-Russian World Championship to be held in its entirety outside the confines of the Soviet Union!

Wheels within wheels. The medieval cosmological view of the harmony of the universe gradually gave way to the Renaissance interpretation, which came much closer to the truth.

OPPOSITE The introduction of artillery in the late medieval period enabled besiegers to break down from a distance the walls of even heavily fortified cities. An analogy in chessboard terms was the new long-range striking power of the queen.

A Greco Game

White: Anonymous
Opponent;
Black: Gioacchino Greco
King's Gambit, played in
1620, venue unknown.

1 e4 e5 **2** f4 f5 **3** exf5 Qh4+
4 g3 Qe7 **5** Qh5+ Kd8
6 fxe5 Qxe5+ **7** Be2 Nf6
8 Qf3 d5 **9** g4 h5 **10** h3
hxg4 **11** hxg4 Rxh1
12 Qxh1 Qg3+ **13** Kd1
Nxg4 **14** Qxd5+ Bd7
15 Nf3 Nf2+ **16** Ke1
Nd3++ **17** Kd1 Qe1+
18 Nxe1 Nf2 smothered mate.

Position after **6** ... Qxe5+

Position after **18** ... Nf2
smothered checkmate

Gioacchino Greco's Primo Modo del Gioco de Partito, *written about 1625. Greco's great service to chess was to make his material available to a wide circle of people.*

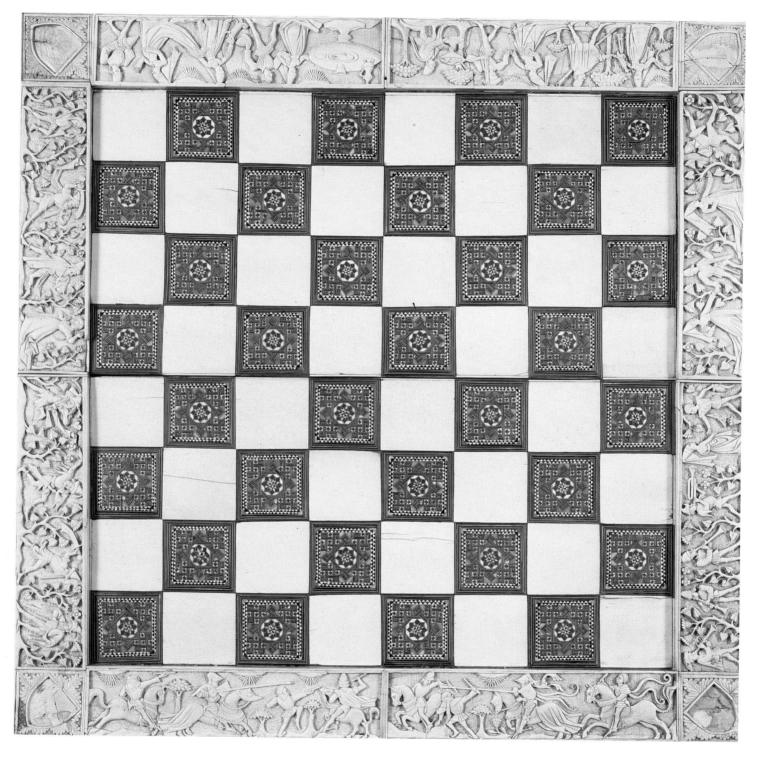

A fifteenth-century French wood and ivory board. The panels of the border indicate that it was for the use of the nobility, with scenes depicting other aristocratic amusements of the period. On one side a joust is in progress, regulated by a marshal with a baton – singularly apt decoration for a chessboard, the battleground for controlled symbolic warfare. Other panels illustrate musicians and dancing, an alfresco banquet and jesters and other entertainers.

This seconde chapitre of the firſt tractate ſheweth who fonde firſt the playe of the cheſſe.

HYS playe fonde a phyloſopher of Thoryent whiche was named in Caldee Exerſes or in greke philometor/ which is as moche to ſaye in engliſh as he that loveth Juſtice and meſure/ And this philoſopher was renomed gretly amonge the grekes and them of Athenes whiche were good clerkys

Two woodcuts from Caxton's Game and Play of the Chesse *(1474). Caxton's book had little to do with chess except as a symbol for morality, rationality and stable social structures. Thus the philosopher teaches the king to play in order to 'correct and reprove*

Columbus discovered the New World for Spain in 1492. It was fitting that the new impetus for chess, as it arose from the slow Arabic and medieval form, should also have come from Spain, ideally placed as that nation was as a centre for world communication in the fifteenth and sixteenth centuries. Ruy Lopez, from Extremadura, a Spanish priest of the sixteenth century, was a leading player of his time. His talent for chess made him internationally famous and he was a favourite at the court of Philip II. In 1560 Lopez, on Church business, visited Rome where he defeated without difficulty the most prominent Italian masters. In all probability, these included the young Leonardo da Cutri. Lopez also worked on a book about chess, which would explain the game to his contemporaries. The result was his *Libro de la Invencion Liberal y Arte del Juego de Axedrez*, published soon after his return to Spain in 1561.

In 1575 the Italians came to Madrid for a return match. Amongst them were da Cutri and Paolo Boi. Matches were arranged with Lopez under the patronage of Philip II. The Spaniards still like to regard this international meeting at Madrid in 1575 as the first real international chess tournament. Nevertheless, this claim does not truly stand up. The games and full results have not been preserved in a way which could enable us to confirm the status of the competition. In spite of the fame of Lopez, through the eponymous

The Openings of the New Chess

King's Gambit

1 e4 e5 **2** f4 – this is the Romantic opening par excellence. White gambits a pawn to break open the 'f' file in order to further his attacking ambitions. Famous practitioners of the gambit include Adolph Anderssen, Bobby Fischer, Boris Spassky and most recently, Judit Polgar. It was mentioned in the earliest surviving printed work on chess, *Repeticion de Amores y Arte de Axedres*, published by Luis Ramirez de Lucena in Spain in 1497.

Lucena's book is divided into two sections, one dealing with chess, the other on love. The chess material includes basic analysis of 10 openings (including the King's Gambit), 150 problems and studies and useful practical advice such as: 'Try to play soon after your opponent has eaten or drunk freely.' This kind of tip seemed prevalent in chess literature of the Renaissance, and might be compared with Ruy Lopez on where to place the chessboard. The other side of the coin can be seen in the advice of Carrera in his book *Il Gioco degli Scacchi* (1617). Carrera suggests this way to prepare for a chess game: 'Abstain some days from meat to clear the brain, as also to let blood . . . take both purgatives and emetics to drive the humours from the body . . . above all be sure to confess sins and receive

spiritual absolution just before play in order to counteract the demoniacal influence of magic spells.'

Lucena is also credited with the authorship of the Göttingen manuscript, a 33-page-long Latin tract which contains similar material to the *Repeticion*. The section on love is actually an attack on feminism. According to *The Oxford Chess Companion*, both love and chess were to Lucena, warfare in miniature.

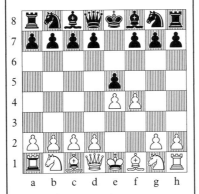

Ruy Lopez

Ruy Lopez was a sixteenth-century Spanish priest, a favourite at the court of King Philip II. In 1561 Lopez published a book of chess openings and general precepts, which included the suggestion that the board be placed so that the sun shines in the eyes of your opponent. The opening moves of the Ruy Lopez (or Spanish) opening are: **1** e4 e5 **2** Nf3 Nc6 **3** Bb5. At this point Black has a wide variety of defences against White's

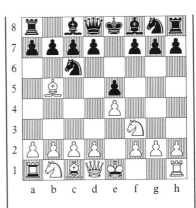

strategy of exerting pressure against the pawn on e5. The Lopez is considered one of the most sophisticated openings and has been a favourite of Steinitz, Capablanca, Fischer and Karpov.

Sicilian Defence

This defence, perhaps the most popular against the king's pawn, commences after the moves **1** e4 c5. Its name stems from the Sicilian priest, Pietro Carrera, who published the defence in 1617. Carrera, not much noted as a player, derives his main claim to fame from his recording of the new openings employed by the Italian masters of the late sixteenth century such as Greco, Polerio and Salvio.

The most ferocious variation of the Sicilian is the Dragon, which arises after the common sequence: **1** e4 c5 **2** Nf3 d6 **3** d4 cxd4 **4** Nxd4 Nf6 **5** Nc3 g6. The name derives from the shape

of Black's pawn structure which is said, fancifully, to resemble the outline of a dragon. More than 25 per cent of all master games are Sicilians, and the vast popularity of this opening resides in the opportunities it grants Black for counterattack, rather than pure defence. Although regarded with suspicion from the 1850s to the mid-1930s, the Sicilian Defence has been championed by Staunton, Botvinnik, Tal, Fischer and Kasparov.

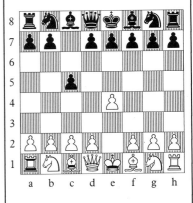

Queen's Gambit

This opening, **1** d4 d5 **2** c4, first became popular in the mid-eighteenth century, as a result of games by Philip Stamma. Stamma was a native of Aleppo in Syria, and according to Harry Golombek, a belated representative of the great Arab school of chess. In 1745 he published *The Noble Game of Chess* in which he strongly advocated use of the

Queen's Gambit. Not surprisingly, this opening originally became known as 'the Gambit of Aleppo'.

Lord Harrington, Stamma's patron in London, helped secure him the appointment of Interpreteur of Oriental Languages by Royal Warrant, dated 14 August 1739 and signed by King George II. This post earned him a salary of £80 per annum. In 1747 in Slaughter's Coffee House in St Martin's Lane, London, Stamma was beaten by eight losses with one win and one draw, by the rising star Philidor. Nevertheless, Stamma's gambit has survived to become the subtle queen's side equivalent of the Ruy Lopez. It has been a favourite of Lasker, Alekhine, Botvinnik and Kasparov.

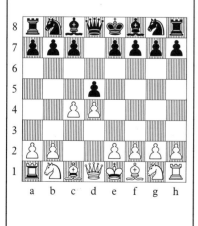

French Defence

1 e4 e6 **2** d4 d5 – this is another defence mentioned by Lucena but it gained its name from a match in 1834 when a Paris team defeated London in a correspondence game. Play normally develops in a closed fashion, with rival pawn chains traversing the centre of the board. Grandmasters who have employed it frequently include Nimzowitsch and Botvinnik.

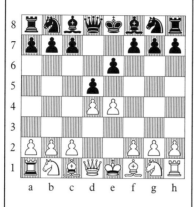

Caro-Kann Defence

1 e4 c6 **2** d4 d5 – this defence has a similar objective to the French Defence, in that Black establishes an immediate foothold in the centre. Nevertheless, the Caro-Kann has one advantage and one disadvantage in relation to its Gallic cousin. The advantage is that the Black queen's bishop is not locked in by its own pawn chain. The drawback is that, having already played … c6, it is more awkward for Black to strike back in the centre with the standard liberating move … c5. The Caro-Kann appeals to strategic players, such as Capablanca,

Botvinnik, Petrosian, Smyslov and Karpov.

The name derives from the British player Horatio Caro (1862–1920) and the Viennese player Marcus Kann (1820–86), whose ideas on this defence were published in the magazine *Bruderschaft*. Nevertheless, as one might expect with such a natural defensive move as **1** … c6, the pedigree is considerably more ancient. In 1590 it was mentioned by Giulio Cesare Polerio (1548–1612), a leading Italian player, regarded for some time as the champion of Rome.

Polerio's manuscripts reveal a meticulous desire to record the most important openings used by the masters of his era. It is a shame, though, that virtually nothing in terms of complete games between identifiable opponents has survived from that time. All that exists are fragments of games, analyses and, at best, brief games where only the name of one player has come down to us.

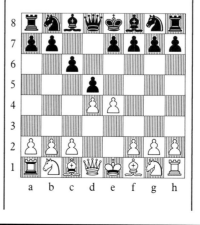

English Opening

1 c4 – this opening move was mentioned by Lucena and by Ruy Lopez, the latter adding the comment that it is so bad that no player of any skill would adopt it. Lopez was wrong! The modern history of the opening, and its name,

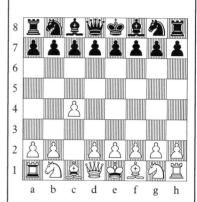

both derive from the use of **1** c4 by Staunton in his 1843 match against Saint Amant in Paris.

Nowadays, the move **1** c4 is normally linked with the fianchetto, or flank development, of White's king's bishop into the g2 square. Strategically sharp positions result, in which White contests the central light squares in vigorous fashion.

Those who have championed the English Opening include Staunton, of course, Réti, Nimzowitsch, Golombek, Botvinnik, Petrosian and, most recently, Kasparov, who added it to his repertoire for the 1987 World Championship match in Seville.

christening of his opening, **1** e4 e5 **2** Nf3 Nc6 **3** Bb5, his playing strength was by no means impressive. If one examines the few extracts of play which have survived from that time, it can safely be said that the general level was abysmal. The players made their moves and hoped for the best. They set out on adventurous excursions with their pieces, more or less punctuated by unforeseen episodes such as fortuitous wins of material or random checks. In particular, giving check to the opposing king seemed to exert an endless fascination on these early practitioners of the chess art. Systematic play simply did not exist. What occurred was mostly a matter of fortune and accident.

The period from Ruy Lopez to Philidor, the first modern master, was bridged by Greco, born around 1600 and active until 1634. Greco's games and analysis were the first to reveal the dynamic movement and potential inherent in the post-Renaissance form of chess. His strategy was still simple, but there was a driving force, a fierce intelligence behind his attacks, which introduced the element of deliberate sacrifice to deliver checkmate to the opposing king. Take, for example, the game on p. 34. The wild opening seems merely to be a series of haphazard checking interludes with both queens. Nevertheless, once Greco succeeds in seizing the initiative on his ninth move, he forces home the attack with great élan.

An engraving by Jacob van der Heyden from Das Schach- oder Königspiel *(Leipzig, 1616). The author, Duke Augustus of Brunswick-Lüneburg, who wrote under the pseudonym of 'Selenus', is shown here sitting on the right. 'Selenus' was generally more famous for this industrious work than for his analysis, which was considered weak.*

B.C.D.
PORTABLE
BOARD

JAQUES, PATENTEE, LONDON.

CHOCOLAT-LOUIT

THE
PROFESSIONALS

O N 9 M A Y 1783 a sensational report circulated in London: 'Yesterday, at the Chess club in Saint James's Street, Mr Philidor performed one of those wonderful exhibitions for which he is so much celebrated. He played at the same time three different games, without seeing either of the tables. His opponents were Count Bruhl, Mr Bowdler, and Mr Maseres. To those who understand chess, this exertion of Mr Philidor's abilities, must appear one of the greatest of which the human memory is susceptible. Mr Philidor sits with his back to the tables, and some gentleman present, who takes his part, informs him of the move of his antagonist, and then, by his direction, plays his pieces.' Philidor, at first a composer of music, later in life made his living from playing chess and writing chess books.

Blindfold chess was not the only revolutionary activity in which this ingenious Frenchman indulged. François-André Danican Philidor (7 September 1726–25 August 1795) dominated those contemporaries of his whom he actually encountered, both over the board and in the realm of chess ideas. Dr Max Euwe has written of Philidor: 'By illustrating his principles in his book *L'Analyse des échecs*, Philidor laid the first stone in the edifice of modern chess.' The revolutionary aspect of all this was the way in which Philidor directed attention towards the essential role to be played by the pawns in chess. Far from being mere cannon fodder for the pieces (as was customary in the games of Philidor's predecessors) the pawns were, in the eyes of this enlightened Frenchman, the very soul or spirit of the game. In his best games Philidor always tried to construct a mighty barricade of pawns in the centre. His opponents often lost because they could not understand what Philidor was trying to do. Some experts have fancifully suggested that Philidor's new theories concerning the paramount importance of the pawns, the Third Estate of the chessboard, were most timely, considering the political events in the France of his day.

The game on p. 45 is typical Philidor. He runs immense tactical risks in the opening in order to build up his favourite pawn centre. Once this has been established, he is invincible, and the position after Black's 29th move represents the apotheosis of his strategy.

The first international chess tournament was organized by the nineteenth-century English polymath, Howard Staunton. Staunton was a typical product of the self-confident Victorian imperial age. His main talent lay as a player of chess; indeed, in 1843 he won a match against the Frenchman, Saint Amant, which elevated him to the position of champion of the chessplaying world of his day. Staunton was, however, not averse to augmenting his income with chess writing, and as his chessboard powers waned, he turned his hand to Shakespearean scholarship and finally, an account of the English public schools.

Staunton was one of the first to recognize the commercial value of product endorsement. Everyone involved in chess has heard of the Staunton pattern chess pieces. They are the most functional and elegant chess pieces available, and for decades they have been the only pieces in use in serious international competitions. Yet Staunton did not design them, he merely lent his name to the pattern of Nathaniel Cooke, a prominent craftsman of the period. To top his other chess ventures, Staunton entered the sphere of chess organization in 1851, exactly coinciding in time and place with the Great London Exhibition, the imperial showcase of Queen Victoria's vast domains.

Staunton's original idea, a first in the history of chess, was to organize an event so attractive that all of Europe's leading players would have no choice but to compete. Staunton's energy and enthusiasm for the project was such that he succeeded in persuading the chess enthusiasts of London to contribute a prize fund of £500, an enormous sum for that

OVERLEAF A German eighteenth-century two-dimensional chess set.

44

A Philidor Game

White: Sheldon;
Black: Philidor
Bishop's Opening,
London 1790.

1 e4 e5 **2** Bc4 c6 **3** Nf3 d5
4 exd5 cxd5 **5** Bb3 Nc6 **6** d4
e4 **7** Ne5 Be6 **8** 0-0 f6
9 Nxc6 bxc6 **10** f3 f5
11 Be3 Nf6 **12** Nd2 Bd6
13 c4 0-0 **14** Ba4 Qc7 **15** f4
Ng4 **16** Qe2 Nxe3 **17** Qxe3
c5 **18** Nb3 dxc4 **19** Nxc5
Bxc5 **20** dxc5 Rac8 **21** c6
Rfd8 **22** Rfd1 Rd3 **23** Rxd3
cxd3 **24** Bb3 Bxb3 **25** axb3
Qb6 **26** Kf2 Qxe3+
27 Kxe3 Rxc6 **28** Rxa7 Rd6
29 Kd2 e3+ **30** Kxe3 d2
31 Ra1 d1=Q White resigns.

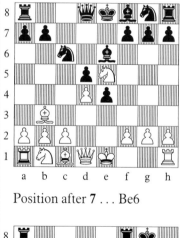

Position after **7** . . . Be6

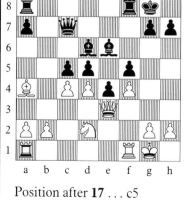

Position after **17** . . . c5

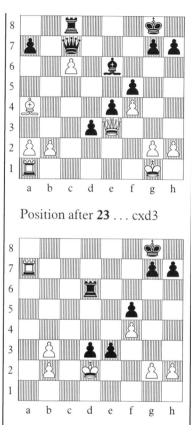

Position after **23** . . . cxd3

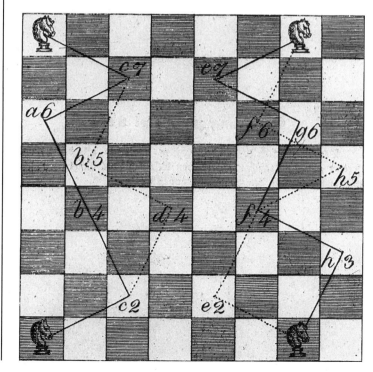

Position after **29** . . . e3+

*ABOVE Philidor, regarded
by many as the first modern
chess master. His books were
universally consulted, but very
few of his games have come
down to us. This portrait
appeared as the frontispiece to
his* Analyse des échecs
(second edition, 1777).

LEFT An illustration from
Mnemonic des Schach-
spieles, *a book teaching people
to play blindfold chess. Not
surprisingly, this concentrates
on the trajectory of the knight,
the most difficult piece for
beginners.*

The Immortal Game

White: Adolph Anderssen; Black: Lionel Kieseritsky King's Bishop's Gambit, Offhand Game, Simpson's-in-the-Strand, London 1851.

1 e4 e5 **2** f4 exf4 **3** Bc4 Qh4+ **4** Kf1 b5 **5** Bxb5 Nf6 **6** Nf3 Qh6 **7** d3 Nh5 **8** Nh4 c6 **9** Nf5 Qg5 **10** g4 cxb5

11 Rg1 Nf6 **12** h4 Qh6 **13** h5 Qg5 **14** Qf3 Ng8 **15** Bxf4 Qf6 **16** Nc3 Bc5 **17** Nd5 Qxb2 **18** Bd6

Qxa1+ **19** Ke2 Bxg1 **20** e5 Na6 **21** Nxg7+ Kd8 **22** Qf6+ Nxf6 **23** Be7 checkmate.

Position after **6** ... Qh6

Position after **12** ... Qg6

Position after **18** ... Qxa1+

Position after **23** Be7 checkmate

Howard Staunton, the first unofficial world champion and a Shakespearean scholar.

These ivory pieces carved by Thomas Staight of Walbrook are based on the theme of Saracens v. Crusaders. They were exhibited at the Great Exhibition of 1851 in London.

THE STAUNTON CHESS-MEN.

BOXWOOD AND EBONY.

ENTERED No. 1402

The original Staunton chessmen, from the pattern book damaged in 1940 by enemy action. They were designed by Nathaniel Cooke and produced by the Jaques Company. Although not designed by Staunton, they were endorsed by him and became the standard pattern for all serious competitions. A remarkable detail is that the elegant knights were based precisely on the horse's head from the Elgin Marbles, which not long before had been put on display in London. These pieces immediately captured the imagination of chess players and have not been surpassed in design to this day.

RIGHT Staunton chessmen. They once belonged to Dr Johannes Zukertort, who played in the first official championship in New York in 1886.

A French set, made in Dieppe, dating from the late eighteenth century. It is also called the 'Bust' set.

Early nineteenth-century Indian pieces. The design is known as the 'Pepys' set because of a similar set in the London Museum.

Chinese pieces manufactured in Macao, and dating from after the Battle of Waterloo in 1815. The king is based on the Duke of Wellington, while the queen is a Chinese image of a European. The third piece is a knight.

OVERLEAF A rare nineteenth-century Indian set in rock crystal, the sides differentiated by ruby or emerald finials. It stands on an eighteenth-century embroidered cloth 'board'.

OVERLEAF, FACING PAGE An Indian late nineteenth-century Vizagapatam ebony and engraved ivory chess table. The board is made of tortoiseshell and ivory, the set of ivory and horn.

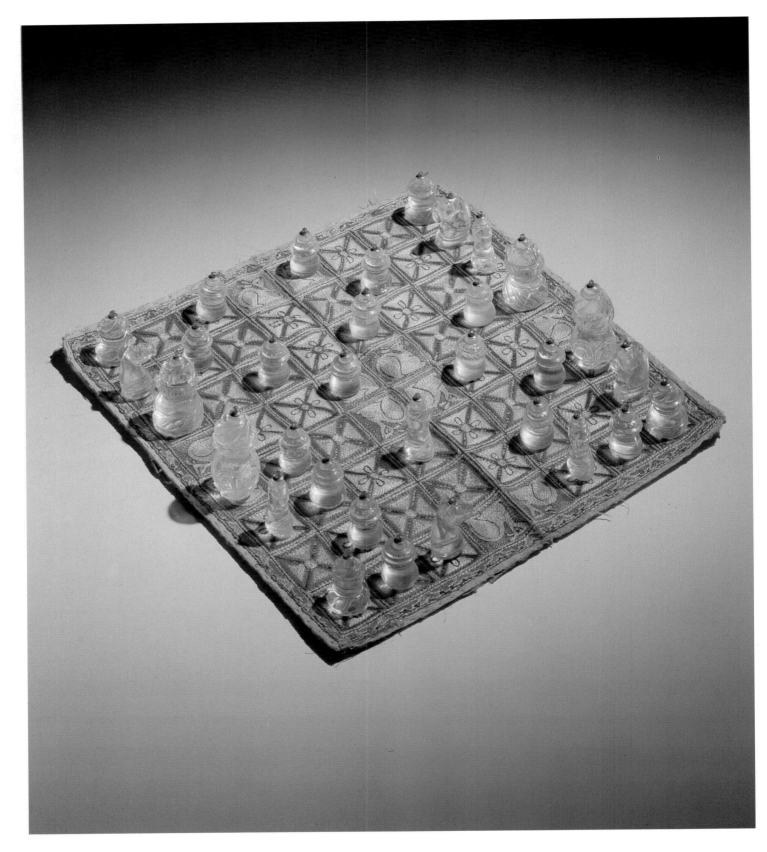

Paul Morphy: The American Meteor

The American genius, Paul Morphy (22 June 1837–10 July 1884), astounded the chess world by his sudden and dramatic appearance in the late 1850s. Morphy was not just well versed in the theory of his day, he was also extraordinarily accurate, possessed complete sight of the board, played rapidly, yet never blundered. Ingenious, resourceful and blessed with outstanding endgame technique, Morphy obliterated the leading masters of his time. When facing Morphy, his opponents seemed weighed down with a cumbrous slowness of a bygone era. As Harry Golombek has noted in a somewhat different context, the contrast between the style of Morphy and that of his major opponents presented the aspect of some antediluvian monsters being annihilated by a modern weapon of destruction.

At the age of 12 in his home town of New Orleans,

Morphy defeated the visiting European master, Lowenthal. This established his fame as a chess prodigy, a curious precursor of his compatriot, Bobby Fischer. Seven years later, Morphy was invited to the first American Chess Congress, held in New York. There he swept the field and defeated another outstanding European master, Louis Paulsen, in the final. The crushing margin of his victory (five wins, two draws and only one loss) combined with the coruscating brilliance of his play, left no doubt that here was a star of the very first magnitude in the chessboard firmament. The game on this page demonstrates with crystal clarity the overwhelming impact Morphy's conduct of his games had on the American chess community.

White: Louis Paulsen;
Black; Paul Morphy
Four Knights' Game, Final,
New York International
Tournament 1857.

LEFT Six years after Staunton's international tournament, the idea spread across the Atlantic. In 1857 in New York the first American Chess Congress was held. To the delight of the home audience first prize was carried off in triumphant style by their own Paul Morphy, who beat the visiting European favourite, the German Louis Paulsen, in the final.

1 e4 e5 **2** Nf3 Nc6 **3** Nc3 Nf6 **4** Bb5 Bc5 **5** 0-0 0-0 **6** Nxe5 Re8 **7** Nxc6 dxc6 **8** Bc4 b5 **9** Be2 Nxe4 **10** Nxe4 Rxe4 **11** Bf3 Re6 **12** c3 Qd3 **13** b4 Bb6 **14** a4 bxa4 **15** Qxa4 Bd7 **16** Ra2 Rae8 **17** Qa6 Qxf3 **18** gxf3 Rg6+ **19** Kh1 Bh3 **20** Rd1 Bg2+ **21** Kg1 Bxf3 dis+ **22** Kf1 Bg2+ **23** Kg1 Bh3 dis+ **24** Kh1 Bxf2 **25** Qf1 Bxf1 **26** Rxf1 Re2 **27** Ra1 Rh6 **28** d4 Be3 White resigns.

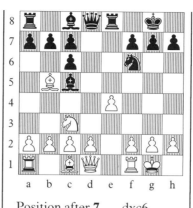

Position after **7** . . . dxc6

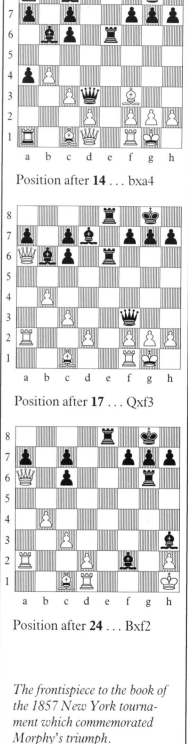

Position after **14** . . . bxa4

Position after **17** . . . Qxf3

Position after **24** . . . Bxf2

The frontispiece to the book of the 1857 New York tournament which commemorated Morphy's triumph.

Simultaneous chess has long
been a popular way for amateurs to meet masters and
grandmasters. The master
progresses around the inside
of rows of players, making
a move on each board as he
passes by. The master here is
M. Rosenthal giving a display
in Paris in the latter part of the
nineteenth century.

OVERLEAF, TOP LEFT
Green and white Russian set
(eighteenth or early nineteenth
century).

OVERLEAF, BOTTOM
LEFT English pocket set from
De La Rue, 1846. The pieces
have studded backs.

OVERLEAF, BOTTOM
CENTRE Chessboard and
pieces for the blind. Note the
raised black squares.

OVERLEAF, TOP
RIGHT Chinese puzzle ball
pieces (nineteenth century) are
decorative novelties rather than
practical games.

OVERLEAF, BOTTOM
RIGHT Counters showing
chess symbols were a con-
venient alternative for front-
line soldiers.

time. This great event commenced in May 1851, and proceeded via a series of knock-out matches, a system for deciding the victor which has declined in popularity in chess contests, but is now the norm for tennis, snooker and many other international sports. The eight prize winners of that momentous occasion, names indelibly engraved in the annals of chess, were: **(1)** Adolph Anderssen (Germany); **(2)** Marmaduke Wyvill MP (England); **(3)** Elijah Williams (England); **(4)** Howard Staunton (England); **(5)** Joseph Szen (Hungary); **(6)** Capt. H. A. Kennedy (England); **(7)** Bernard Horwitz (Germany); **(8)** J. R. Mucklow (England).

Staunton celebrated his great organizational triumph by publishing his account of the tournament in Bohn's Scientific Library in 1852. The book was simply called *The Chess Tournament*. There had been no event like this before and this book ushered in a new era of international competitive chess. It was the precursor of modern grandmaster tournaments and of the modern World Championship cycle itself. The intense enthusiasm for this new project, of the greatest players of the age, can be assessed from the following extract from a letter by the Hungarian master, Szen, in which he accepts the invitation. 'When the news reached me of the approaching Exhibition of the World's Industry, and of the Chess Tournament connected with it, there arose within me an irrepressible desire to tread once more the soil of England, whose inhabitants have already realized such truly noble ideas, that they may with right and justice, sing Rule Britannia. Then awoke in me also my old passion for Chess, and this so strongly, that if the Committee, having regard to my slight reputation, think me worthy of it, I shall consider myself happy and honoured in co-operating according to the best of my abilities in the great World-contest.'

The game on p. 48, by the victor of the London Tournament, was actually played in Simpson's-in-the-Strand, the coffee and cigar divan, beloved of the chess fraternity of the day. This was a genuine 'coffee house' game, of the sort often played for cash stakes. In this game, the vanquished player was so impressed with the brilliance of execution of his opponent's attack, that he immediately dashed to the nearest telegraph office to transmit the game to the Café de la Régence in Paris, the Gallic equivalent of Simpson's. From that day on, this brilliant exploit has earned the sobriquet, 'The Immortal Game'.

Encouraged by his triumph on his home territory, Morphy left in 1858 for a European tour. In a series of matches in London and Paris he overwhelmed Lowenthal (again), Harrwitz and finally, the great Adolph Anderssen himself, the champion from London 1851. Again, the margin of Morphy's superiority was astonishing. Anderssen won two games and drew two, but lost seven. Had anyone thought of creating a world champion title at that time, Morphy would surely have been the laureate.

Morphy's prodigious infancy foreshadowed that of Bobby Fischer. Morphy's sudden withdrawal also provides an eerie precedent for Fischer's abandoning of chess. After beating Anderssen, Morphy played no more matches, or indeed games, against first-class opponents, confining himself to simultaneous displays and casual games with inferior opponents. To these he habitually gave heavy odds. Morphy became increasingly eccentric, developed paranoiac delusions and ultimately refused even to talk about chess. He died in 1884, of apoplexy. As with Fischer, Morphy's vanishing act, at or near the height of his powers, imbued him with legendary, superhuman powers in the eyes of the public. In spite of the slender corpus of competition games (75) he has left, many against opponents not worthy of his steel, the belief persists that Morphy may have been the greatest genius chess has ever seen.

MODERN TOURNAMENTS

S INCE London 1851, tournaments have come a long way. Several of the techniques developed by international players for tournament success are described on the following pages. It should be repeated, though, that Staunton's knock-out system has largely been replaced, nowadays, by all-play-all competitions and Swiss systems. In the latter, hundreds of players, ranging from the elite to enthusiastic amateurs, can play together in a limited number of rounds, possibly even in as short a time as a weekend. Knock-outs are now, more or less, restricted to the qualifying groups of the World Championship cycle.

Chess, as played in contemporary tournaments, is assuming more and more the aspect of a sport. I now divide the sporting influences under three important headings: the chess clock, analysis of adjourned games and the scientific investigation of openings theory.

All serious games of chess are nowadays subject to a time control. Every player has, for example, to complete 40 moves in two hours, or in speed games, all the moves in 30 minutes. Failure to complete the moves in the allotted time results in the draconian punishment of loss of the game by time forfeit. Even world champions are not immune to such an indignity. In the famous eighth game of their World Championship match at London in 1986, Anatoly Karpov lost on time with no less than ten moves still to make against Gary Kasparov. But this was not always the case.

Time controls were first introduced in 1861 for the match between Anderssen and Kolisch. Previously, unlimited licence to ponder moves was open to abuse. Thus, it was reported that Paul Morphy was almost driven to tears by the excessively slow play of his opponent, Louis Paulsen. Staunton's famous criticism of Williams provides another example: 'Uses hours over moves when minutes would suffice.' Staunton went on to accuse Williams of boring his opponents to death, not outplaying them.

Originally, sand glasses were employed to measure the use of thinking time. At the Great Tournament of London 1883 the 'chess clock' as such made its debut. These early chess clocks operated on the pendulum method and the change to the modern push-button variety occurred gradually between 1895 and 1900.

The modern tournament chess clock consists of two normal clock faces joined together, but each clock only operates when a button on the opposite clock is pushed downwards. The key difference from a standard clock face is that each chess clock is equipped with a small metal flag by the numeral 12. The advancing clock hand raises this flag as it approaches 12, but the flag falls instantly the moving hand has passed that number. When the flag falls, if a player has not made the requisite number of moves, he loses on time. After each player has made his move, he pushes the button on his own clock. This halts its motion, while automatically starting that of his opponent.

The chess clock can prove a mighty weapon in the practical struggle. Several grandmasters, such as Mecking, Browne or Korchnoi, indulge in exaggeratedly nerve-wracking demonstrations during time trouble which can have the effect of screwing up the tension. This may, of course, not be intentional. These grandmasters, and others like them, may find that the adrenalin only flows when they are involved in cliff-hanging time scrambles to beat the clock. The introduction of a physical element into an ostensibly intellectual activity often has the effect of disconcerting the opponent. Common practices in this time-trouble battle of nerves consist, for example, in panic-stricken staring at the clock, bouncing up and down in one's chair and thumping the clock down hard when a move is made.

This chessboard and photograph are on display in the bar of Simpson's-in-the-Strand, which used to be the most celebrated chess haunt in London. Notables from the past look down from their portraits on an assemblage of great players in London in 1888, including Zukertort and Steinitz (second row 4th and 5th from right).

Mecking, the Brazilian grandmaster, was also famous for holding down his hand firmly during time scrambles to prevent his opponent from pressing the clock. This happened, to my knowledge, in a game from the Hastings international tournament of 1972. Mecking's opponent, not unnaturally, was the one to lose by time forfeit. One might with justice ask, though, where was the umpire at the time? The Romanian grandmaster, Gheorghiu, not to be outdone, executes baroque flourishes with his pieces during time trouble. He brandishes the pieces wildly in the air before bringing them down with a thunderous crash onto the board. I once saw him hurl a rook so vigorously onto the chessboard that it bounced off and ricocheted onto his opponent's head. Gheorghiu adds to this amazing performance by slamming the clock button, as if he were a sledgehammer, after his move. He has very clearly realized the role to be played by sound effects in modern tournaments. If it is possible to create a noise resembling the repeated explosions of fire crackers during the game it will naturally impede the opponent's ability to think.

Wilhelm Steinitz, the first official world champion. Steinitz earned his living not just as a professional chess player but also by his prolific and often acerbic use of his pen in widespread chess publications.

Crossplay of the Strongest Tournaments ever held

AVRO (named after the sponsors, a Dutch radio station) was played on the peripatetic system, the first round being played in the Grand Hotel Krasnopolsky, Amsterdam, with subsequent rounds in Breda, Utrecht, Haarlem and so on. After AVRO the method went out of fashion. Inevitably the older players (Alekhine, Capablanca) were handicapped to an extent and spoiled some positions near the end of the first session. It was obvious that trekking all over Holland unduly favoured the stamina of the younger grandmasters, Keres, Fine and Botvinnik. Botvinnik himself later wrote: 'One cannot help recalling the intolerable tournament programme. On the playing days the participants often had to do without dinner. The time was spent on trains, the event being held in many Dutch towns. It is little wonder that the oldest participant, Capablanca, finished in last but one place.'

In spite of the difficult conditions a substantial number of the AVRO games have been recognized as classics.

AVRO 1938 in the Netherlands

	F	*K*	*B*	*A*	*E*	*R*	*C*	*F*	*Pts*
Fine	●	0½	1½	11	10	10	½½	1½	**8½**
Keres	1½	●	½½	½½	½½	1½	1½	½½	**8½**
Botvinnik	0½	½½	●	1½	½0	1½	½1	½½	**7½**
Alekhine	00	½½	0½	●	1½	½½	½1	½1	**7**
Euwe	01	½½	½1	0½	●	0½	01	1½	**7**
Reshevsky	01	0½	0½	½½	1½	●	½½	1½	**7**
Capablanca	½½	0½	½0	½0	10	½½	●	½1	**6**
Flohr	0½	½½	½½	½0	0½	0½	½0	●	**4½**

The 1948 World Championship

	B	*S*	*K*	*R*	*E*	
Botvinnik	●●●●	½½1½½	11110	1½011	1½1½½	**14**
Smyslov	½½0½½	●●●●	00½1½	½½1½½	11011	**11**
Keres	00001	11½0½	●●●●	0½10½	1½111	**10½**
Reshevsky	0½100	½½0½½	1½01½	●●●●	1½½11	**10½**
Euwe	0½0½½	00100	0½000	0½½00	●●●●	**4**

A tense moment during a club competition in Moscow. The player in the lefthand corner represents the team from the state broadcasting corporation, Gostelradio.

It can be seen, therefore, that for some contemporary grandmasters chess is less a refined intellectual pursuit, than outright war. It should be added, though, that the majority of leading players are perfect gentlemen at the board, no matter how aggressive their private intentions may be.

When Howard Staunton defeated Saint Amant in their match at Paris in 1843, the task of the respective helpers or seconds, as they were known, was to provide moral, not analytical, support. It was rare that adjournments were allowed in this 21-game clash and the games often extended for seven hours without pause. In modern tournaments and World Championship matches the situation is quite different. Games which have not already been decided, are adjourned after five or six hours and resumed after a period which may either be two hours or, indeed, several days. At World Championship level, each player is assisted by an entire team of seconds, coaches and analysts, who may, during the overnight pause, dissect an adjourned position to the extent that perfect play may result for ten or even twenty moves when the game is resumed the following day.

Not unnaturally, this element of analysis by seconds has aroused criticism. Why should others be able to intervene in a game between two players? Although the practice has been widespread since the late 1930s, future rule changes may perhaps phase this out. One possible solution is to speed up the time limits so that more moves are caried out in the initial session of play. That would have the effect of terminating most games before the adjournment stage was reached.

For modern tournament and match play exhaustive advance preparation is regarded as an integral part of the struggle. With hundreds of tournaments on the national and international level taking place every year, the standard of knowledge, plus the rate of acquiring that knowledge, is constantly being raised. Additionally, analytical investigation into key lines of modern openings theory is constantly being published in an unstemmable flow of chess books, specialist magazines and now, computer-based data archives. No fully equipped modern grandmaster would dare to arrive at an important competition nowadays without his portable computer and his chess data base, containing many thousands of significant games in its electronic memory banks.

This massive flow of up-to-the-minute information has resulted in very deep research into certain opening variations and also against types of opening employed by specific opponents. The openings knowledge of most modern grandmasters is astronomical, in comparison with that of their nineteenth-century precursors. It can even happen that a player may win a game, on the basic contours of another game, which has already been played, before he has left the paths of his own before-game analysis.

If one were to ask the proverbial man on the Clapham omnibus (or, indeed, on the New York subway) whether he knew more about Morphy or Petrosian, or whether he had heard of Petrosian at all, I am sure I would know the answer. Nevertheless, Petrosian was world chess champion for six years, while Morphy was just a legendary genius who never held the title. The official matches for the World Championship began with the contest between Steinitz and Zukertort in 1886. But these two chess Titans were preceded by numerous talented players, worthy of a World Championship title, which did not exist at that time.

The most prominent amongst these were the Frenchmen Philidor and Labourdonnais, the Englishman Staunton, the German Anderssen and Morphy himself, the meteor of American chess. Still, it was not until the Austrian Jew Wilhelm Steinitz declared himself

68

champion, that the title officially came into existence. It is his name which is the first to go into the annals of the world chess champions. By defeating Zukertort in 1886, Steinitz silenced any opposition to his bold, and hitherto, unprecedented claim.

The world champions who took the title before the foundation of FIDE (the World Chess Federation) in 1924 were: Wilhelm Steinitz (Austria/USA) 1886–94; Emanuel Lasker (Germany 1894–1921; José Capablanca (Cuba) 1921–27. At this time the world title was the private property of the reigning champion. There was no way to force a champion to defend his title, but the double spur of honour and money ensured reasonable frequency of title defences. No one had an automatic right to a challenge, but if a potentially successful gladiator appeared, he could usually reckon on obtaining adequate financial support for an attempt on the chess throne. This free-market system did not function too badly, but evinced obvious weaknesses which exposed it to justifiable criticism.

Some title matches simply consisted of a rather meaningless lap of honour for the champion and took place solely because an inadequate challenger had fortuitously drummed up a tolerable level of monetary support. In this category was the second match, in 1910, between Lasker and Janowsky. Other matches, which the chess world would have dearly loved to witness, never occurred. Perhaps the intended challenger could not raise the right

Under the remote gaze of a picture of Steinitz, Emanuel Lasker faces Harry Nelson Pillsbury in a game in 1896 in St Petersburg. Pillsbury was defeated, but eight years later, playing the same opening, produced a new move which he had worked out in the intervening period, flooring Lasker and giving himself his long-delayed revenge.

Knightmare! A selection of eighteenth- and nineteenth-century knights.

A Capablanca Game

White: Ossip Bernstein; Black: José Capablanca Queen's Gambit Declined, Exhibition Game, Moscow 1914.

1 d4 d5 **2** c4 e6 **3** Nf3 Nf6 **4** Nc3 Be7 **5** Bg5 0-0 **6** e3 Nbd7 **7** Rac1 b6 **8** cxd5 exd5 **9** Qa4 Bb7 **10** Ba6 Bxa6 **11** Qxa6 c5 **12** Bxf6

Nxf6 **13** dxc5 bxc[...] Qb6 **15** Qe2 c4 [...] Rfd8 **17** Nd4 Bb[...] Rac8 **19** bxc4 dxc4 **20** Rc2 Bxc3 **21** Rxc3 Nd5 **22** Rc2

24 Nb3 **26** Nb5 **28** Rxc3 Rxc3 **29** Rxc3 Qb2 White resigns.

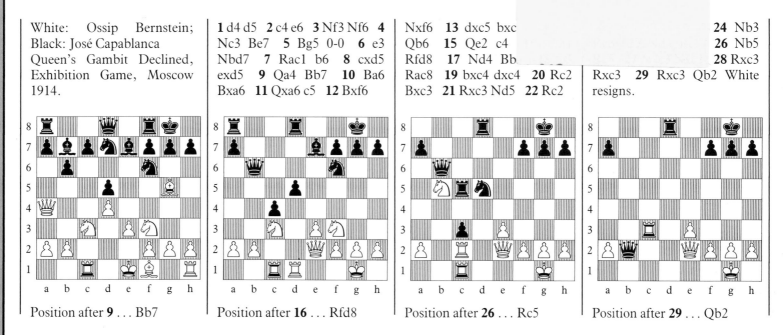

Position after **9** ... Bb7   Position after **16** ... Rfd8   Position after **26** ... Rc5   Position after **29** ... Qb2

A young genius at play. The four-year-old Capablanca confronts his father. Note the father has the comfortable chair!

One of the strongest tournaments ever held, St Petersburg 1914 was packed with the immortals of the game. It was the last great triumph of Lasker (front row, third from left), before World War I put an end to tournament activity. Nimzowitsch (back row, fourth from left) clearly was not attending to the photographer. Marshall (back row, second from left) sent the picture with its scribbled notes to his wife.

finance, or perhaps, the champion deflected a challenge by insisting on exaggerated conditions. In 1927 Capablanca lost the title to the Franco-Russian genius, Alekhine. Throughout the 1930s, chess enthusiasts worldwide eagerly awaited a revenge match between Alekhine and Capablanca. But it never took place. Alekhine busied himself with clashes against lesser mortals, such as Euwe and Bogoljubow.

When Alekhine died in 1946, reduced to alcoholism and poverty in post-war Lisbon, FIDE seized its chance to take over the control and organization of the World Championship. Alekhine had been the first champion to die in possession of the title. FIDE employed the interregnum to arrange a tournament of the world's five strongest grandmasters. This was won by Botvinnik (ahead of Smyslov, Reshevsky, Keres and Euwe). FIDE decreed that the champion, henceforth, would have to defend his title after a given period of years (initially three) against a challenger, thrown up by a global series of carefully regulated qualifying events.

The World Championship cycle, as this came to be known, ensured that a champion's laurels could not wither while he slumbered on them. Additionally, dethroned emperors of the chess world could always stage a comeback, should they have the strength to fight their way through to a renewed match. This was an option, or rather a right, which simply did not exist for Capablanca.

At first, in the early 1950s, when the initial FIDE-regulated championship defence took

place (Botvinnik-Bronstein, Moscow 1951) champions enjoyed an automatic right to a rematch, without the necessity of slogging through the qualifying tournaments. This clause became known as the Botvinnik Rule, since he profited from it twice to win back the title. In 1963 this somewhat unfair privilege was abolished, only for it to be reintroduced in 1977 for the newly crowned champion, Anatoly Karpov. Now that Gary Kasparov holds the sceptre, the right to a return match has once again been rescinded. One might legitimately ask whether the disappearance and return of this right are purely fortuitous.

Before FIDE took control, private negotiations between the contestants and their backers determined the conditions under which the matches were fought out. Sometimes it was a question of scoring a majority of points from a given maximum number of games. At other times the victor was the man who first scored a specific total of victories in individual games. The length of matches varied wildly between ten games (as in Lasker-Schlechter 1910) and 34 games (as in Capablanca-Alekhine 1927). Between 1951 and 1972 FIDE standardized the conditions of victory. All the matches were to last a total of 24 games. The first player to score $12\frac{1}{2}$ points would win the title. If the result were 12-12 (which actually occurred with Botvinnik-Bronstein 1951 and Botvinnik-Smyslov 1954) the defending champion retained the title.

The world champions who came to power after 1924, when FIDE was founded, though still, until 1946, relatively powerless, were: Alexander Alekhine (Russia/France) 1927–35, 1937–46; Max Euwe (Holland) 1935–37; Mikhail Botvinnik (USSR) 1948–57,

PRECEDING PAGES A praiseworthy attempt to assimilate chess into popular culture in cigarette cards of the 1930s.

The backs of the cards (RIGHT) incorporate quite advanced information about the game.

A wry, Bunteresque look at school chess in the 1930s. However, the Boy's Own Paper *took chess very seriously as can be seen from their own portable chess set distributed with the paper.*

76

HERALDIC SIGNS & THEIR ORIGIN.

A SERIES OF 25 Nº 21

WILL'S CIGARETTES

THE CHESS-ROOK.

There are few objects of household life in use before the end of the sixteenth century of which instances cannot be found as charges upon coats of arms. The "chess-rook" is a well-known heraldic figure, although it has been suggested from the conventional form which is always adopted, that it is by no means certain that the intention was to represent the chess-man. In the shield depicted however there can be no doubt as to this intention, for the arms are those of the family of Rocke of Clungunford, and the intended pun is obvious.

W.D.& H.O. WILLS, Bristol & London

ISSUED BY THE IMPERIAL TOBACCO COMPANY
(OF GREAT BRITAIN & IRELAND), LIMITED.

CHAMPIONS OF 1936

A SERIES OF 50

14

DR. MAX EUWE

Chess Champion of the World

Dr. Max Euwe, a tall, bespectacled professor of mathematics at Amsterdam University, is the Chess Champion of the world. He won the title on Dec. 15th, 1935, by beating Dr. Alekhine in a series of 30 games. Dr. Alekhine, the famous Russian player, had been champion since 1927, and he beat Dr. Euwe in the Masters' Tournament at Nottingham Chess Congress in Aug., 1936, but that did not affect the title. The new champion is a believer in perfect physical fitness and he declares that it is impossible to play chess efficiently unless you are healthy. He regards swimming and tennis as ideal exercises.

ISSUED BY
· OGDEN'S ·
BRANCH OF THE IMPERIAL TOBACCO CO.
(OF GREAT BRITAIN & IRELAND), LTD.

BRITISH CHAMPIONS OF 1923

SERIES OF 75

J. R. Capablanca.

Greatest of all chess players. Champion of the world in 1923, having opposed fifty players at once.

5
ISSUED BY
GALLAHER LTD
BELFAST & LONDON.

TURF CIGARETTES

SPORTS RECORDS

Second Series, Nos. 26-50

34.—CHESS.

Our picture illustrates the astounding feat accomplished by Sir George A. Thomas, Bart., who successfully played against no less than 32 different opponents at the same time.

Alexander Boguslavsky Ltd.
55, PICCADILLY LONDON. W.

BRITISH CHAMPIONS OF 1923

SERIES OF 75

Lady Chess Champion.

Miss Price, British Lady Chess Champion, who was successful in nearly all her matches held at the Hastings Chess Congress.

26
ISSUED BY
GALLAHER LTD
BELFAST & LONDON.

CHAMPIONS

Base Ball.	Isaac Murphy, Jockey.
Andrews, (C.F.Philadelphia).	Charles Wood, do.
Anson, (1st Base, Chicago).	Beeckman, Lawn Tennis
Brouthers, (1st Base, Detroit).	Dwight, do.
Caruthers, (P. Brooklyn).	Sears, do.
Dunlap, (Capt. Pittsburgh).	Taylor, do.
Glasscock, (S.S.Indianapolis).	Marksman.
Keefe, (P. New York).	Captain Bogardus.
Kelly, (C. Boston).	Beach, Oarsman.
Prince, Bicyclist.	Jake Gaudaur, do.
Rowe, do.	Hanlan, do.
Stevens, do.	Teemer, do.
Wood, do.	James Albert, Pedestrian.
Daly, Billiards.	Pat Fitzgerald, do.
Schaefer, do.	Rowell, do.
Sexton, do.	Dorn, Pool.
Slosson, do.	Jack Dempsey, Pugilist
Vignaux, do.	Jake Kilrain, do.
Broadswordsman.	Mitchell, do.
Duncan C.Ross,	Jem Smith, do.
Capt. Mackenzie, Chess	Sullivan, do.
Steinitz, do.	Myers, Runner.
Zukertort, do.	Strongest Man in the World.
Foot Ball.	Emil Voss.
Beecher, (Capt.of Yale Team).	Wild West Hunter.
W. Byrd, H.ge, High Jumper.	"Buffalo Bill."
"Snapper" Garrison, Jockey.	Joe Acton, Wrestler.
McLaughlin, do.	Muldoon, do.

GOODWIN & CO.
NEW YORK.

DO YOU KNOW?

A SERIES OF 25

No. 24 ABOUT CHESS

Chess is the greatest of all board games. This is a diagram of the board, with pieces indicated by their equivalents in chess notation, at the beginning of a game. The symbol for each piece is opposite the square it normally occupies or, in the case of the pawns, at either end of the pawn-row.

Issued by

RINGTONS LIMITED
HEAD OFFICE
ALGERNON ROAD NEWCASTLE UPON TYNE 6

1958–60, 1961–63; Vassily Smyslov (USSR) 1957–58; Mikhail Tal (USSR) 1960–61; Tigran Petrosian (USSR) 1963–69; Boris Spassky (USSR/France) 1969–72; Robert Fischer (USA) 1972–75; Anatoly Karpov (USSR) 1975–85; and Gary Kasparov (USSR) 1985–.

From 1978 until 1984 FIDE determined that the victor in each match would be the first person to register six wins. The first game of the Karpov-Korchnoi clash in 1978 took place in the Philippine city of Baguio. For six years previously there had been no World Championship, not since the famous battle between Spassky and Fischer at Reykjavik in 1972. By despatching Boris Spassky, Fischer finally smashed the Soviet monopoly which had been in place since 1948.

Fischer's was a curious case. No sooner had he stormed the chess Olympus in the most highly publicized match of all time, than he renounced chess totally. Fischer has not played a single serious game of chess since Reykjavik 1972, and the prognosis, even though he is still a relatively young man, for his re-entry into the competitive arena, is extremely poor. In 1975 Fischer refused to defend his title. FIDE, therefore, declared Anatoly Karpov the new champion, the only one in the history of chess to become champion by default. This unfortunate outcome was, however, manifestly not the fault of the young Russian.

To most observers Fischer's conduct was, at best, dereliction of duty to the chess-loving public and, at worst, deranged. Yet Fischer's withdrawal was in one sense comprehensible. Having once scaled the summit of a mental Everest, there is a psychological resistance against performing such a feat for a second time. Fischer appears to have seen himself as 'World Champion' in an absolute way. He, therefore, experienced no need to demonstrate this fact again. Those champions of the past who have descended into the hurly-burly to defend their hard-won titles have, by ultimately suffering defeat at the hands of the most worthy challenger, compromised their invincible reputations. By totally isolating himself, Fischer, in a remarkable parallel to his compatriot, Paul Morphy, created a myth of chessboard omnipotence. Achievement, however, cannot be allowed to stagnate. In spite of his mythic status, the real world passed Fischer by, a lonely figure on his distant peak.

If many observers had held Karpov to be a paper tiger when he took the title without a struggle in 1975, his subsequent achievements over the following ten years shamed his critics and established his reputation as one of the best and most conscientious of world champions. In a decade he twice defended the world title in matches, took part in the strongest tournaments and seized a record number of first prizes. It was only in 1985 that any shadow clouded his achievement. This came to pass in his marathon 48-game collision with Kasparov, which stretched over five months from late 1984 to early 1985.

Karpov, having taken a near-decisive lead in a first to win six games contest against his young rival, Gary Kasparov, ultimately failed to secure victory. The match was eventually halted 'without result' by the World Chess Federation. There followed a period of confusion in the regulations which witnessed an unprecedented number of World Championship matches, an incredible four in just a three-year period. During this time, when the rules were in perpetual flux, virtually all systems to determine a winner were tried out. Having governed world chess since 1948, FIDE found its hegemony threatened by dissatisfied grandmasters, who formed their own union, the Grandmaster Association, to restore order to the chaos.

Nineteenth-century women at chess. The International Tournament of London.

Heading this, as its first president, was the self-same Gary Kasparov, who finally dethroned Karpov in 1985, and clung to the title through two rematches in 1986 and 1987. The turmoil surrounding the chess crown now resembles nothing so much as a chessboard version of the confused dynastic strife of the Wars of the Roses: on the one hand Kasparov, on the other, Florencio Campomanes, the ruling president of FIDE, the man who stopped the first match between Karpov and Kasparov.

From 1886 the history of the game of chess itself is very much bound up with, and determined by, the personal history of the official champions of the game and those great challengers who sought to wrest the title from them. To the chess enthusiast, and even the man

A portrait gallery of grandmasters who formed the elite in the 1880s and early 1890s. Wilhelm Steinitz, the first world champion (*TOP LEFT*), beat off challenges from the brilliant Prussian Johannes Zukertort (*BOTTOM RIGHT*) and Mikhail Tchigorin (*BOTTOM LEFT*), the founder of the Russian school of chess. Dr Siegbert Tarrasch (*TOP RIGHT*) avoided challenging Steinitz for the world title, but his match with Tchigorin in 1893 was regarded as the apogee of chess at that time. A German, Tarrasch was the great chess teacher of the classical school.

in the street, names like Capablanca, Fischer, Spassky conjured up idols with mythic mental powers. For the chess expert, their games very much determined the direction and fashion of the playing styles of their time.

Since official championships began just over a century ago, just 13 men have held the supreme chess title, that of world champion. Wilhelm Steinitz (17 May 1836–12 August 1900) was the first man to become official world chess champion, holding the title from 1886 to 1894. He was the most profound thinker on the strategic plane that the game had ever seen, although his rivals, Zukertort and Tchigorin, somewhat outshone him in the area of complex combinations and attacks. Nevertheless, his deep understanding of defensive play (some experts have claimed that Steinitz's defensive barricades were the chessboard foreshadowing of the trench warfare which became the norm during World War I) and his philosophy of victory through the accumulation of small advantages, influenced an entire generation of grandmasters. Indeed, his own contemporaries, faced by his new strategy, were often left in bewildered defeat when facing the Austrian genius. If Paul Morphy had shown precisely how 'open' positions should be handled, it was Steinitz who illuminated the correct paths in the infinitely more subtle 'closed' openings.

Born in Prague, Steinitz moved in 1858 to Vienna and represented Austria in his first international tournament at London in 1862. Thereafter, he took the decision to reside in London which at that time was rapidly becoming the capital of world chess. Frequent great tournaments were held there in the decades following Staunton's experiment of 1851. On top of that, chess centres, such as Simpson's-in-the-Strand, formed a natural focus and meeting point for all the world's leading players. Simpson's, the most famous of these centres, was a natural, if vast, extension of the chess-playing coffee houses of the eighteenth century. It was known as a 'chess and cigar divan'; there amateurs could challenge the great masters for a stake, matches and tournaments were held and the enthusiast could catch up on the latest games and publications. It, and others like it, very much resembled a chess version of the celebrated London gentlemen's clubs. Indeed, the Immortal Game between Anderssen and Kieseritsky, was played at Simpson's as an offhand game in 1851. Steinitz rapidly became a denizen, and challenges from amateurs helped to augment his income.

While in London Steinitz dominated British chess, not entirely to the liking of his chosen compatriots. In 1866 he won a match against Anderssen, the victor of London 1851, and he went on to crush Bird and Blackburne, two of the leading English masters, in set contests. *The Field* magazine, perhaps an unlikely place for a chess column to be found, nevertheless recognized Steinitz's merits and invited him to contribute regular articles. These were models of how games should be described and explained.

In the early 1880s it became apparent that Steinitz's main rival was the Prussian Zukertort, who had won the London 1883 tournament ahead of him. Both men, fierce rivals on and off the board, claimed the World Championship, a title which had never before been recognized. In 1886 the matter was decided in a three-venue match in the USA. Steinitz, in spite of a very poor start, triumphed with ten wins to five with five drawn games. Having demolished his sole rival, Steinitz bestrode the world of the 64 squares like a colossus, while Zukertort, demoralized and broken in health, died two years later. Over the next few years, now domiciled in the USA, Steinitz swept aside challenges from the European grandmasters, Tchigorin and Gunsberg. But in time, age caught up with the man who had become world champion at the age of 50.

In 1894 the young Emanuel Lasker (24 December 1868–11 January 1941) inflicted a painful defeat on the old champion, winning by almost the same score as Steinitz had against Zukertort at the inception of his reign. A return match, held in Moscow two years later, resulted in utter humiliation for the veteran. It would have been better for his peace of mind had he not entered this new contest. Steinitz was briefly interned in a psychiatric institute in Moscow, recovered his health and for some years remained a dangerous tournament opponent. But in 1900 illness seized him anew, and he died, in utter poverty, in New York. The memory of Steinitz's destitute final months has haunted masters of the game ever since. It was to have a bitter echo in the final days of Alexander Alekhine, the third man after Steinitz to hold the championship.

Lasker was world champion from 1894 until 1921. No one has ever succeeded in holding the title for a longer period, nor is it likely that anyone ever will. Even after he had lost the title, Lasker still celebrated important tournament victories and at the age of 67, a virtually incredible gerontological feat, he was still competing successfully in world class events.

Lasker's play has always fascinated experts. Some accused him of bewitching or hypnotizing his hapless victims. How else could it be explained that he was able to slaughter outstanding grandmasters in droves, as he did? In reality, Lasker was the perfect fighter, revelling in the struggle, possessed of amazingly subtle understanding and blessed with immense reserves of physical and psychological energy. Against difficult opponents he rejoiced in a fight to the death on the edge of the precipice, and more often than not, it was his opponent who went hurtling to his doom.

Lasker was born in Prussia and rapidly made his name in tournaments and matches in Germany, England and the USA from 1889 to 1893. The following year came his big chance, a match against Steinitz. Many regarded Lasker as inexperienced, but during the course of the contest Lasker became the master, soaking up knowledge and tactics as he went along, while Steinitz was relegated to the role of pupil.

Once champion, Lasker recorded the most sensational series of first prizes in grandmaster tournaments. At St Petersburg 1895/96, Nuremberg later the same year, London 1899 and Paris 1900, Lasker reduced the world's leading grandmasters to apparent novices. As if finding chess too simple, Lasker now withdrew for several years into a profound study of mathematics and philosophy. Finally, however, in 1908 he re-emerged to defend his title in a series of matches against formidable opponents, Tarrasch, Schlechter, Marshall and Janowsky. His final great tournament result as champion came at St Petersburg 1914, where he also bested the most prominent grandmasters of the younger generation, Capablanca and Alekhine. Lasker ultimately lost the title in a 1921 challenge from Capablanca held in Havana. The old champion, his finances, health and nerves undermined by four years of war in Germany, was unable to do himself justice and did not win a single game against the Cuban virtuoso.

Once he had lost the title, Lasker's appearances dwindled. He did win the great tournament of New York 1924, once again finishing ahead of his younger rivals, Capablanca and Alekhine. It was at this tournament that Lasker created an entirely new branch of endgame theory, showing that in certain special circumstances, a lone knight may draw against the opponent's rook and pawn, an astonishing discovery. Ten years later, Lasker, a Jew by origin, was forced yet again to enter the tournament arena, merely to earn his living. The advent of the Nazis in Germany had made him an exile from his homeland. For some years he wandered around the world, competing at Zürich, Nottingham and Mos-

Schach! Schach!

A German political cartoon from the World War I period. Germany and Austria, clearly enjoying overwhelming superiority on the chessboard, deal invincible check to the appalled Anglo-French-Russian-Italian alliance.

cow. For a man of his age, the results were outstanding, including wins against Capablanca and against Euwe, whom he defeated twice. In 1941 Lasker died in New York.

José Raoul Capablanca (19 November 1888–8 March 1942) was perhaps the first modern chess player to become a superstar. When he lost a game to Richard Réti at New York in 1924 he had previously gone an incredible eight years without a single defeat. The loss against Réti made headlines around the world. Capablanca had been considered invincible, an iron man, a magician of the chessboard.

Capablanca was born in Havana and held the World Championship for six years from 1921 to 1927. He picked up the moves of the game, so the legend goes, at the age of four, watching his father play with friends. When he was 12 Capablanca overcame the resistance of the Cuban champion, Corzo, in a set match, and the myth grew when in 1909 he absolutely annihilated America's leading grandmaster and one of the world's top players, Frank Marshall. This devastating match victory had a curious follow-up. Solely on the basis of that win, Capablanca was invited to the grandmaster tournament of San Sebastian 1911. This was a somewhat stuffed-shirt affair, where all the contestants were meant to have won first prize in at least one grandmaster tournament. Two of the contestants, established members of the 'Grandmaster Club' (Nimzowitsch and Bernstein), protested against the invitation to the young Cuban. The mythology rapidly engulfing Capablanca required that he should destroy both of the protesters in his games against them, and carry off undivided first prize ahead of the world's best. Both of these feats, of course, Capablanca accomplished with ease.

In 1913 Capablanca obtained a position in the Cuban Foreign Office which opened up to him unlimited possibilities for foreign travel and hence for chess. Eight years later, the Capablanca legend was crowned when he won the World Championship, in his home city, from Lasker. Capablanca became, thereby, the only man in the history of chess not to lose a single game while winning the World Championship.

Throughout the mid-1920s, Capablanca's tournament record was neither so active nor so imposing as his legend might have demanded. Nevertheless, at New York in 1927, ahead of all his main challengers, the Cuban registered one of the most complete tournament victories of all time. Yet again, in the course of this magnificent triumph, he did not lose a single game. The myth of invincibility appeared intact, so imagine the universal shock when Capablanca was toppled from his throne some months later by the buccaneering challenge from the younger Alekhine. For this match, held over several months in Buenos Aires, the normally aggressive Alekhine switched his style, in opportunistic fashion, to heavy-duty strategic chess in the manner of his opponent. After a marathon war of attrition, from which Alekhine emerged with six wins, three losses and the staggering total of 25 draws, Capablanca conceded victory on 29 November 1927, just ten days after his 39th birthday.

Capablanca never obtained the chance for a return match, although he continued to turn in outstanding tournament results to demonstrate himself the most eligible challenger. In 1942 in the Manhattan Chess Club, New York, the Cuban genius died of a heart attack. Alekhine wrote that the chess world 'would never see his like again'. Of his games, it has been declared that they breathe 'a serenity, a crystal clarity, a perfection which is the result of the highest art'.

The game on p. 72 is a wonderful illustration of Capablanca's genius. Black's 29th move, which annihilates White's resistance at a stroke, was hailed at the time as a 'thunderbolt'.

Alexander Alekhine (1 November 1892–24 March 1946) was the first man to win the World Championship twice. The first time was in his battle of Titans against Capablanca in 1927. Thereafter, for eight years, Alekhine dominated the chess landscape in a way which had not been seen since the best days of Emanuel Lasker. If it was impossible to beat Capablanca, it was even more difficult not to lose to Alekhine. Senior grandmasters, such as Aron Nimzowitsch, lamented that Alekhine bowled them over like children. Unbridled success, however, went to Alekhine's head. Unable to derive sufficient stimulation from the chessboard, he switched to the blandishments of alcohol. More or less in a perpetual stupor, Alekhine lost his title to the Dutchman Max Euwe in 1935.

Defeat exerted a salutory lesson on this wayward genius. Unlike Capablanca in 1927, Alekhine had wisely insisted on a return match clause in his contract with Euwe. Suppressing his predilection for hard liquor, Alekhine became a devotee of milk products, and in his newly sober state, regained the title with some ease from the selfsame Euwe in 1937. Without ever defending the title again, Alekhine stayed as champion until his death in 1946. Of course, World War II made the organization of international chess rather difficult, and it was hardly Alekhine's fault that he did not defend the title after 1937.

Alekhine's career was one long adventure, both on and off the chessboard. His games

Scarcity of decent opposition in the trenches. The fox is clearly winning!

Sketch by Paul Weber, 'Anyone for Chess, Little Red Riding Hood?' or 'What big pieces you have, Grandma!'

abounded in risk, brilliant ideas, but also dreadful mistakes. His books of best games have become Bibles for aspiring young masters. Gary Kasparov, himself, has proclaimed that Alekhine, 'whose attacks came like thunder from a clear sky,' was his model. Legend has it that Alekhine's family in Tzarist Russia was of the minor aristocracy. In 1914, when war broke out, our hero was playing in a tournament in Mannheim, and was promptly interned as a hostile alien. Regaining his freedom, he returned to Russia and served on the Austrian front, it is said in the medical corps. Here he was wounded. After the Russian Revolution he appears to have been arrested and, once more, was forced to escape, first to Switzerland and then to Paris. Film actor . . . Doctor at Law from the Sorbonne in Paris . . . who knows? Alekhine's personal curriculum vitae hinted at both, but the hard evidence is scarce. Suffice it to say, that Alekhine became the most brilliantly aggressive chess master the world had ever seen.

During World War II Alekhine fell into Nazi clutches. He participated with great distinction in numerous tournaments in occupied Europe, and simultaneously fell under suspicion of having penned anti-Jewish articles in chess magazines, casting aspersions on the creative ability of Jewish grandmasters. It was somehow a fitting symbol of Alekhine's turbulent existence that he should have died in Estoril, just outside Lisbon, at the end of the war, amongst the colonies which had congregated there of displaced European royalty, aristocrats and stranded German spies. Ironically for the champion, broken in health and once again submerged in mind-numbing fumes of alcohol, the news was on its way that England was prepared to stage a challenge match with the rising Soviet star, Mikhail Botvinnik. This challenge would have restored Alekhine's fortunes, even had he lost. This, in spite of his vast powers of determination and recuperation, would have been the most likely outcome.

Dr Max Euwe, (20 May 1901–26 November 1981), the fifth world champion, suffered from two handicaps. In the first place, he was the first genuine amateur to win the world title. Then, World War II, during which his home country, the Netherlands, suffered particular privations, unfortunately coincided with what should have been his most creative and productive years.

We have already seen how he first won the championship from Alekhine, only to lose it back a mere two years later. After the war and the occupation of Holland by the Nazis were over, Euwe emerged once more into the tournament fray. At the Groningen tournament of 1946 he registered a colossal result, second only to Botvinnik, but ahead of a galaxy of the strongest grandmasters. But two years later, disaster struck. At the 1948 Five-Man Match Tournament for the World Championship, designed to terminate the interregnum following Alekhine's death, Euwe came a pathetic last. This buried, once and for all, any realistic hope he may have harboured of regaining the title he had held so briefly.

It was typical of the man, once he could no longer aspire to the highest honours over the chessboard, that he should still strive for the most important post available in the world-wide chess fraternity. In 1970 he was elected President of the World Chess Federation, FIDE, only retiring, voluntarily, in 1978. Euwe was a prolific author and theoretician of the game. His direct, forceful and logical style influenced the entire younger generation of Dutch masters and grandmasters. Alekhine described Euwe as 'the man who never missed a combination.' Indeed, Euwe's success in wresting the title from Alekhine, on the Dutchman's home ground in 1935, had the effect of making chess virtually the national sport in his country.

SOVIET HEGEMONY – WESTERN CHALLENGE

'Chess is the gymnasium
of the mind'
(Lenin)

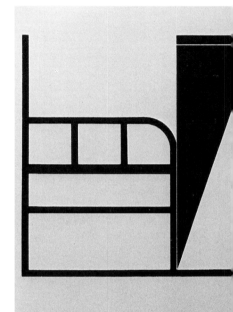

T HE first Soviet citizen to hold the World Championship was Mikhail Botvinnik (17 August 1911–). In that sense, he might be seen as the progenitor of a dynasty. Since 1948, when Botvinnik acceded to the purple, all world champions have been Soviet Russians, except for a brief incursion by Bobby Fischer. Chess had been supported by the Soviet state since the mid-1920s. Botvinnik, and most of his Soviet successors as champions, enjoyed the immense back-up state support initially implies. However, they also suffered its limitations. These became painfully clear, for example to Karpov and Kasparov, when they were forced to hand over to the Soviet sports committee the bulk of their foreign currency earnings from their otherwise immensely lucrative world-title bouts.

Botvinnik had the unique distinction of winning the title on no less than three occasions, in 1948, again in 1958, when he regained the title from Vassily Smyslov, and once more in 1961, when he repeated this feat against Mikhail Tal. Although Botvinnik retained the championship, on and off, for a period stretching over 15 years, he never succeeded in dominating the chess environment in the way that Steinitz, Lasker, Capablanca and Alekhine had done in their day. In this sense, he was regarded very much as 'primus inter pares', rather than an absolute dominator of the game. This phenomenon can be explained by recourse to the immense upsurge in the quantity of top-class grandmasters, all ready to dispute the palm with the champion, whenever the latter should enter tournament lists. The pattern set by Botvinnik, of being regarded while champion as first

LEFT The Russian reformer and novelist Count Leo Tolstoy defending the King's Gambit. He wears peasant dress, in contrast to his more conventionally clad opponent.

PRECEDING PAGE A Russian eighteenth-century king, made in Kholomogory of walrus ivory.

RIGHT Lenin practising his dialectical skills against A. Bugdanov. Gorky (wearing hat, hand on chin) watches the game with rapt attention.

ABOVE Rodchenko's 1925 design for a chess table and chairs for the Workers' Club. Rodchenko said of these designs: 'Almost all the pieces are built on a dynamic principle so that you can open out an object in a small space to work and put it back compactly afterwards. I consider this principle to be a characteristic typical of and inherent in contemporary work.'

amongst equals, persisted amongst his successors, Smyslov, Tal, Petrosian and Spassky. It was believed by experts that the champion, given the general rise in knowledge about the game, could in fact, no longer excel in the manner of the old masters.

Botvinnik himself was largely responsible for this rise. His training methods, research and iron logic became the norm. Botvinnik stressed that the secret of his genius lay in immense preparation and intensive investigation of theoretical possibilities, just as much as in inspiration over the board. He regularly published his ideas, which included the concept, novel at the time, that chess was a sport which required iron physical as well as mental discipline. For example, Botvinnik detested tobacco. Therefore, he arranged private training games, during the course of which his opponents were encouraged to blow smoke into his eyes. It might have been simpler to persuade FIDE to ban smoking during tournaments, which has, in fact, now come to pass.

Botvinnik's longevity on the chess throne, combined with his ability to strike back from adversity, to regain his title twice, will live forever in the annals of chess history. Nevertheless, the belief, current in his day, that the world champion could no longer dominate his turbulent rivals, has been proven false, as we shall see in the careers of Anatoly Karpov and Gary Kasparov.

An early twentieth-century chess set from Russia, typifying all strata of tsarist Russian life, from the peasantry to the Cossacks, from the Orthodox Church to the tsar himself. The pawns wear Russian regional costumes.

Soviet miners in a workers' club enjoy a game of chess against a painted backdrop showing the new Soviet man exercising his brains (having exercised his body) in an idyllic pastoral setting.

Vassily Smyslov (24 March 1921–), world champion from 1957 to 1958, once wrote a book of his best games with the title *In Search of Harmony in Chess*. This is singularly appropriate. Smyslov was not only one of the strongest grandmasters the world has ever seen, he was also an opera singer of outstanding qualities, once auditioning for a singing role in the Bolshoi Theatre, Moscow. Fortunately for chess, Smyslov failed the audition, but he is always happy to burst into song on chess occasions at the slightest provocation.

During the 1950s, Smyslov dominated the qualifying events which led up to a challenge against Botvinnik. Nevertheless, his three matches with Botvinnik for the title were inconclusive. The first, in 1954, was drawn; Smyslov won at the second attempt in 1957, but just one year later, he fell victim to the somewhat unfair return match clause, and Botvinnik was crowned as champion once more.

Smyslov's playing style was calm, Olympian, almost aloof. He shunned confusing tactics, always preferring a pristine, strategic path. Perhaps, this approach, designed as it was, to minimize nervous tension, helps to explain Smyslov's immense gerontological feats which outshine even those of Emanuel Lasker. Given that modern chess is a strenuous sport, and is recognized as such by many governments around the world, it was truly amazing that in 1984, at the age of 63, Smyslov could have penetrated to the final of the qualifying competition to determine a challenger to world champion Anatoly Karpov. It was no disgrace that Smyslov should have succumbed in that qualifying match to the rampant young genius, Kasparov.

Universally known as the 'Magician from Riga', Mikhail Tal (9 November 1936–) took the chess world by storm in the late 1950s. In his seemingly inexorable headlong rush to the chess throne, he demolished every grandmaster in sight. When he even toppled the mighty Botvinnik in their match at Moscow in 1960, it seemed that the glorious days of Capablanca or Alekhine had returned. Tal's results were not simply brilliant, his games were replete with coruscating tactical complexities which left opponents and commentators utterly baffled. One grandmaster, Pal Benko, even came to a game against Tal wearing dark glasses, to ward off supposed hypnotic rays emanating from the fiercely dark eyes of the young sorcerer.

Sadly, the vision was soon shattered. Within months of his winning the title, it became clear that Tal was seriously ill with kidney disease. In the inevitable revenge match against Botvinnik in 1961, an ailing Tal, a shadow of his former self, was slaughtered. Tal remained, and remains, a formidable opponent, but for two decades he has had no realistic prospect of fighting his way back to the pinnacle of championship chess. Still, at blitz chess, with five minutes for each player for the entire game, Tal continues to shine. Blitz does not demand the stamina required for the grind of tournament or match chess, hence it is ideally suited to Tal's present condition. In the 1988 World Blitz Championship at St John, Canada, Tal delighted his many supporters by winning first prize ahead of both Karpov and Kasparov!

In 1963 Mikhail Botvinnik was finally deposed as world champion by the Armenian Tigran Petrosian (17 June 1929–13 August 1984). The veteran's right to a revenge match, which he had exploited to regain the title from Smyslov in 1958 and Tal in 1961, had been abolished by FIDE. Petrosian, therefore, was secure as champion for a full three years. In 1966 the wily Armenian went one step further. By defeating Boris Spassky, he became the first incumbent world champion for 32 years to win a World Championship match outright against a challenger.

The United States team, guests in Moscow for the 1946 match against the Soviet side. Several members of the American team, such as Reshevsky (front left), had emigrated to the United States from Eastern Europe during the 1920s.

Petrosian was the stylistic antithesis of Tal. Where Tal revelled in unfathomable complexities and wild, barbaric, sacrificial rites, Petrosian, possessed of a highly refined sense of danger and eel-like, slippery defensive skills, steered for lengthy, risk-free battles of manoeuvre. Although Petrosian, when provoked, was able to produce jewels of chess strategy, all too often his detestation of any kind of risk led to colourless games, where the glorious tactical opportunities were inexorably relegated to footnotes in sub-variations to the game commentary.

Petrosian ultimately shed his title to a renewed challenge from Spassky in 1969. A mere 15 years later, when there was still much good chess left in him, Petrosian was snatched away by a sudden illness. With Petrosian's demise, chess enthusiasts lamented the loss of what might have been. One always had the feeling that, had he stirred himself, Petrosian would have been capable of so much more.

With Boris Spassky (30 January 1937–), the sense of waste is even greater, perhaps, than with Petrosian, for Spassky, in his early years, suffered no inhibitions which might have restrained his genius. Where Petrosian sought to consolidate, Spassky, his near-contemporary, loved to attack. When Spassky defeated Petrosian in their match at Moscow in 1969, it seemed that he had nothing but a bright and glorious future ahead of him. Sadly, this was not so.

The very first challenge to Spassky's reign came from the mercurial American, Bobby Fischer. Subjected to the harsh glare of the world's media, Spassky went down to defeat in a match which transcended a purely chessboard conflict. The clash between American grandmaster and Soviet champion inevitably assumed political and symbolic overtones, which could not have been welcome to the vanquished.

The battering which Spassky received, sadly knocked the guts out of him. He never succeeded in staging a world title comeback and, indeed, in his homeland his reputation was swiftly obscured by that of the rising star, Karpov. The restrictions of Soviet life began to irk Spassky's free spirit. Within years he emigrated from the Soviet Union and now resides in France, a nation he also represents in the chess Olympics. His tournament results, his élan quenched by Fischer's onslaught, are now littered with the debris of countless anodyne games, agreed drawn without a proper struggle. Spassky is now a prime example of a once bold warrior converted to pacifism.

Bobby Fischer (9 March 1943–) is the enigma of chess. The story of the teenager from Brooklyn, New York, who developed chess genius with such speed that he was able to topple the entire Soviet chess empire before his 30th birthday, is the stuff of myth and legend. Indeed, the musical *Chess* (Tim Rice and Abba), which ran on the London stage from 1986 to 1989, was largely inspired by Fischer's exploits. At Reykjavik in 1972 (the first World Championship match to be held outside Moscow for over two decades) in the most publicized chess event in the history of the game, Fischer achieved his dream and deposed Boris Spassky. The young American thus became the eleventh world champion.

Here is the result of that historic match (1 indicates a win; 0 a loss; $\frac{1}{2}$ means that the game was drawn).

World Championship, Reykjavik 1972

Spassky $1/1/0/\frac{1}{2}/0/0/\frac{1}{2}/0/\frac{1}{2}/0/1/\frac{1}{2}/0/\frac{1}{2}/\frac{1}{2}/\frac{1}{2}/\frac{1}{2}/\frac{1}{2}/\frac{1}{2}/\frac{1}{2}/0$

Fischer $0/0/1/\frac{1}{2}/1/1/\frac{1}{2}/1/\frac{1}{2}/1/0/\frac{1}{2}/1/\frac{1}{2}/\frac{1}{2}/\frac{1}{2}/\frac{1}{2}/\frac{1}{2}/\frac{1}{2}/\frac{1}{2}/1$

ABOVE Jubilant Armenians hail the victory of their national hero Tigran ('the Tiger') Petrosian as he returns home to Erevan after winning the 1963 World Championship in Moscow.

Never ones to do anything by halves, Soviet officials crown Botvinnik as world champion in Moscow in 1951 (RIGHT). Nine years later Mikhail Tal (FAR RIGHT) wrested the crown from Botvinnik. The laurel wreath had grown even larger in the interval!

Chess in Art

BELOW Detail from Chess Players *by Daumier.*
Petit Palais, Paris

RIGHT Detail from The Chess Players *by Bill Jacklin.*
Private collection.

Chess in Art

Board games have figured in art from the earliest days of city civilization. The ancient Egyptians used senet in representations of the pleasures of everyday life. It also played a significant role in funerary illustrations: the human player had to win since he was armed with the correct incantations in order to pass this success to the other world.

More recently, artists have used chess to convey a specific social milieu. Thus, Indian miniaturists or Arab illustrators have adopted chess to suggest an opulent quality of civilized urban life. In the West, Medieval manuscripts have employed chess to symbolize the many virtues of chivalry or, a topic to which chess naturally lends itself, the union of opposites in courtly love.

In the post-Renaissance period, chess has been employed by artists such as Cornelis de Man (page 38), Jan de Bray (half-title) and Honoré Daumier (page 98) to imply a certain type of sitter or an emotion such as calm, contemplation or agitation. Chess is here used as a vehicle to express a mood.

In the twentieth-century, Paul Klee, Vasily Kandinsky, Juan Gris and Max Ernst (page 102) have been attracted to chess motifs in their abstract work. No doubt, the strict formality of the 64 squares appeals to the modern sense of mathematical abstraction.

However, the most celebrated and greatest modern artist to work repeatedly with chess themes is Marcel Duchamp. He was a strong chess player in his own right and played on second board for the French national team behind only the world champion Dr Alexander Alekhine. Duchamp's treatment of chess is virtually a microcosm of twentieth-century art. He began in 1911 with *Portrait of Chess Players* (page 103), a purely figurative work depicting two players engrossed in the game. He proceeded via Cubist designs in the second decade of the century to conceptual representations of the conflict between two sides, inherent in chess, in such works as *The Large Glass*, perhaps the most profound and enigmatic construction of the century. Later, Duchamp also turned to chess equivalents of found objects (objets trouvés); one such is simply a framed record of a chess game played in 1928.

There is boundless scope in abstraction for the representation of mythological and historical themes within a fixed and readily recognizable framework. Chess sets similarly provide, within clear frames of reference, vast opportunities for working in any material from metal to moulded bread.

BOTTOM On the conventional board Black's queen sacrifice forces checkmate next move, but on Escher's metamorphic planes the White king can escape downwards.

RIGHT Detail from Chess Board, *etching (1920) of infinite planes of chessboards by Jacques Villon, brother of Marcel Duchamp.*

BELOW E. McKnight Kauffer's costume for the White Queen in the ballet Checkmate *1937.*

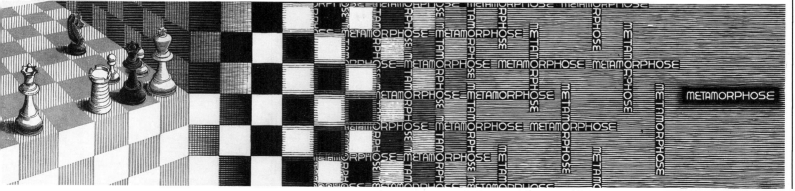

Chess in Art

BELOW '*The King Playing with the Queen*'. *The bronze sculpture (1944, cast 1954) by Max Ernst led him to create a metal chess set in similar style, with which Duchamp enjoyed playing.*

RIGHT '*Portrait of Chess Players*' *(1911) by Marcel Duchamp. Duchamp captured better than anyone else the intense reflection and isolated concentration required in chess.*

Fischer won the title with the magnificent score of 12½ points to Spassky's 8½. The game on p. 105 was instrumental in establishing Fischer's ascendancy in the match. It is appalling that Fischer has not played a single serious game of chess since the final game of the Reykjavik match. In the subsequent 18 years, numerous efforts have been made to lure the reclusive genius back into the game, but to little effect. A common remark in chess circles is that Fischer has become the Loch Ness Monster of chess, often sighted but never seen.

The popular image of chess has tended to be that of an intensely cerebral activity. In comparison with stars from other sports – football, tennis, golf or snooker – grandmasters have exerted a limited public appeal beyond the circles of the game's devotees. The Soviet domination of chess has done much to reinforce this view. Yet chess can be real news, chess masters can command huge fees, they can become superstars and millions of fans around the world can hang on the result of their matches. All this came about very largely as a result of Bobby Fischer's impact on the game. His exploits and adventures, on and off the chessboard, created world headlines and showed that chess was a game of action, rewarding individual effort, an international sport for young people, not just a matter for abstruse debate amongst bespectacled Soviet intellectuals.

During the 1950s, champions, such as Botvinnik and Smyslov, struggled for the supreme chess title with a few thousand roubles as their potential financial reward. In 1987 the prize fund at the Kasparov-Karpov match in Seville was no less than £1.2 million. That was a development instigated by Fischer's insistence that chessplayers should be remunerated on a similar scale to other top sportsmen. It was not just the brilliance of Fischer's play, the textbook models of chess strategy and tactics which he produced that justified his material demands. It was also his determination to make chess as exciting as possible by playing every game to the utmost limit of his possibilities. All this catapulted chess into an entirely new league. It was tragic that Fischer himself was no longer around to benefit.

There is a great deal of political satire concealed in Sir John Tenniel's illustrations for the chessboard world of Alice through the Looking Glass *(B E L O W). The Red Queen was an eccentric employer: 'Jam yesterday, jam tomorrow, but never jam today' were her normal terms of payment. As* The Times *cartoon (A B O V E) shows, the message was still a potent one in the 1980s.*

On 24 April 1975 Anatoly Karpov (23 May 1951–) became the twelfth world champion, and the first to receive his title by forfeit. This was not his fault, however. Fischer simply refused to play. En route to his aborted challenge match, the young Russian had overcome the resistance of grandmasters such as Polugaievsky, Spassky and Korchnoi. Once champion, Karpov threw himself with such energy into justifying his new status, that he ultimately established a record for winning first prizes in tournaments, which is never likely to be broken (Karpov has won around 80 tournaments). If, during the Botvinnik era, the champion was merely seen as a kind of senior colleague in the chess common room, Karpov made every effort to establish his right to sole and autocratic rule in the kingdom of chess. His example was a good one, for his successor, Gary Kasparov, has also done his maximum to emulate Karpov in this respect.

In the absence of Fischer, Karpov sought out all other main rivals prepared to face him. Twice, in 1978 and 1981, he beat off challenges from the great Victor Korchnoi. Only after Karpov had held the title for a decade did he meet his Waterloo at the hand of Kasparov, a young Azerbaijani, in a marathon series of matches, the most colossal battle for the championship the world has ever seen.

Spassky v. Fischer

White: Boris Spassky;
Black: Bobby Fischer
Nimzo-Indian Defence, 5th
Game World Championship
Match, Reykjavik 1972.

1 d4 Nf6 **2** c4 e6 **3** Nc3
Bb4 **4** Nf3 c5 **5** e3 Nc6
6 Bd3 Bxc3+ **7** bxc3 d6
8 e4 e5 **9** d5 Ne7 **10** Nh4
h6 **11** f4 Ng6 **12** Nxg6
fxg6 **13** fxe5 dxe5 **14** Be3
b6 **15** 0-0 0-0 **16** a4 a5
17 Rb1 Bd7 **18** Rb2 Rb8
19 Rbf2 Qe7 **20** Bc2 g5
21 Bd2 Qe8 **22** Be1 Qg6
23 Qd3 Nh5 **24** Rxf8+
Rxf8 **25** Rxf8+ Kxf8
26 Bd1 Nf4 **27** Qc2 Bxa4
White resigns. A terrible
debacle for the then world
champion. After **28** Qxa4
Qxe4 Black has the dual
threat of . . . Qxe1 checkmate
and . . . Qxg2 checkmate.
Should White seek to parry
this with **29** Kf2 then **29** . . .
Nd3+ is disastrous for him.

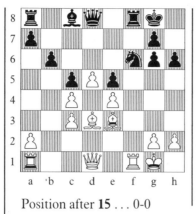

Position after **15** . . . 0-0

Position after **23** . . . Nh5

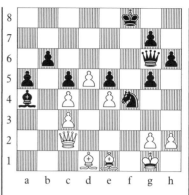

Position after **27** . . . Bxa4

*L E F T Bobby Fischer, car-
icatured here as part archetyp-
ical capitalist, part Western
cowboy, challenges the Soviet
hero Boris Spassky for his
world title in Reykjavik in
1972. The scene is littered with
stunned officials, overworked
advisers and one happy backer
in the shape of British million-
aire Jim Slater, lending a help-
ing hand with Fischer's sack of
assorted currencies. The man
looking in the wrong direction
is Dr Max Euwe, then President of FIDE.*

Position after **7** . . . d6

*R I G H T Peter Brooks' Spec-
tator cartoon fantasizes on the
fact that Deep Thought, the
world's top chess computer, is
partly funded by the Pentagon.*

Karpov's playing style appears effortless. He is able to reduce complex tactical problems to seemingly simple, strategic formulae. He is not a great analyst of the game, nor a deep theoretician. Instead, his forte is in continuous play. More than any other champion, Karpov seems to love playing chess for its own sake. He is intoxicated with the thrill of the game.

Gary Kasparov (13 April 1963–) became the youngest world champion in the history of competitive chess, when, on 9 November 1985 in Moscow, he won the 24th and final game of his second match against Karpov. The World Chess Federation issues, twice a year, a ranking list of all international players. The highest rating previously achieved was that of Bobby Fischer in 1972, at 2785. Kasparov has now smashed that record by reaching 2810, while Karpov, roused by the challenge of Kasparov, has reached a new personal peak of 2755, and he is straining at the leash to increase this. These three players together dominate the all-time world ranking list. As an indication of the extent of their supremacy, a candidate for the World Championship would come out at around 2650, while 2500 plus is grandmaster level, and an international master, of whom there are fewer than one thousand in the world, would be 2400.

Professor Arpad Elo, the originator of the ranking system, has calculated that other top champions, such as Alekhine, Botvinnik, Lasker and Capablanca, range, on his system, from 2690 to 2725.

The drastic game on p. 112 made it clear to everyone that a new champion was on the threshold.

Who can challenge the seemingly invincible duopoly of Kasparov and Karpov? Will it be England's Matthew Sadler, at 15 the youngest male international master in the world? Or the slightly older Michael Adams, already a grandmaster at the age of 17? Perhaps it will be France's Joel Lautier, victor of the 1988 Junior World Championship, or that fierce young Russian, Vassily Ivanchuck. What are the prospects of the first female, absolute world champion? Judit Polgar (Hungary) is only 13, as I write, and the youngest international master in the history of the game! But will the challenge necessarily come from a human player at all? For this intriguing possibility, see the next chapter.

Some grandmasters stand out by their play, others, by their teaching and their books. I will conclude this chapter by looking at three great chess pedagogues, whose influence was disseminated as much, if not more, by their writing, as by their games.

Dr Siegbert Tarrasch (5 March 1862–17 February 1934) was known as the Praeceptor Germaniae, the supreme doctrinaire of the German school. In the early 1890s he was almost certainly the world's strongest player, but he neglected to challenge the ageing Steinitz, and when Lasker won the world title in 1894, Tarrasch's opportunity had gone.

Tarrasch promulgated clarity and logic on the chessboard, laying stress on swift mobilization, occupation of the centre with pawns and active play for the pieces, even at the cost of structural weaknesses. Tarrasch was, in fact, the epitome of the classical grandmaster, and his theories and writings took chess as far as it could go along that very direct, powerful, yet simple path.

Before World War I Tarrasch was the teacher, not just of Germany, but of the whole world. His undying reputation rests on such great books of exposition as *Dreihundert Schachpartien* (Leipzig 1895) and *Die Moderne Schachpartie* (Leipzig 1912) as well as his indefatigable production of chess columns and articles. At this time, Tarrasch's position as chess professor seemed unchallengeable. But just as the old European order was swept

This modern interpretation of the traditional chess set emphasizes the elegance of simple folded paper form.

The Hypermodern Openings

Réti's Opening

1 Nf3 – Although this move had reputedly been played by Napoleon, such games are generally deemed to be apocryphal. Zukertort used the move in the nineteenth century, but mainly as a method of transposing to a kind of delayed Queen's Gambit. It was only the contribution of the hypermodern grandmaster Richard Réti (28 May 1889–6 June 1929) during the 1920s, which welded **1** Nf3 into a distinct system.

Réti demonstrated that **1** Nf3 could lead into some of the most subtle and sophisticated positions on the chessboard. He held back his central pawns, while exerting pressure on the opponent's camp from fianchettoed long-range bishops operating from bases on b2 and g2. In 1924 at New York, Réti created a sensation, defeating none other than Capablanca with his new opening. This was the first game Capablanca had lost for eight years. Capablanca himself immediately became a convert to the opening. Others who followed in his path were Botvinnik, Smyslov and Petrosian.

King's Indian Defence

The key moves of this defence are **1** d4 Nf6 **2** c4 g6 **3** Nc3 Bg7 **4** e4 d6. The King's Indian is evidently an even more extreme version of delayed central occupation than the Nimzo-Indian. In fact, in the early stages, White is allowed more or less a free hand, since Black hopes to strike back with a later counterattack based on the twin thrusts . . . c5 or . . . e5.

One of the earliest examples of the King's Indian occurred in the game Cochrane v. the Brahmin, Moheshunder Bonnerjee, played in Calcutta around 1847. Louis Paulsen also championed this defence, but it remained generally unfashionable and was considered virtually unsound until the 1940s. At that time, Soviet grandmasters, notably Bronstein, revived the King's Indian and imbued it with many dynamic counterattacking ideas. In recent decades it has proved most popular with aggressive players such as Tal, Fischer and Kasparov. Players of a more classical bent, for example, Spassky and Karpov, have, however, tended to shun it.

Nimzo-Indian Defence

The Nimzo-Indian is as popular against **1** d4 as is the Sicilian against **1** e4. The defence is named after, and was indeed invented by, the Latvian grandmaster, Aron Nimzowitsch. Nimzowitsch was active mainly during the 1920s and early 1930s and for much of this time was considered a candidate for the World Championship. Nimzowitsch belonged to the hypermodern school which held, amongst other tenets, that control of the centre need not derive solely from occupation with pawns. An acceptable alternative lay in permitting one's opponent to construct a strong pawn centre, which could then be undermined. The opening moves of the Nimzo-Indian (or Nimzowitsch-Indian, in its full form) are **1** d4 Nf6 **2** c4 e6 **3** Nc3 Bb4. It is evident from this sequence that part of Black's undermining process will consist of inflicting targets on White's pawn structure by playing . . . Bxc3+ at some point to double White's pawns in the 'c' file. The so-called 'Indian' defences were introduced mainly during the 1920s. The appellation refers to a supposed resemblance to the Indian form of chess where players hold back the moves of their central pawns. The Nimzo-Indian is one of the most popular openings, numbering amongst its adherents Botvinnik, Capablanca, Fischer and Karpov.

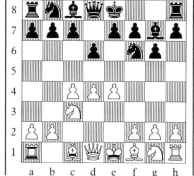

Boris Spassky, world champion 1969–72, contemplates.

ABOVE Michael Adams, aged 17, became the world's youngest grandmaster in summer 1989.

ABOVE RIGHT Will she topple Kasparov? Judit Polgar, aged 12 in this 1988 picture, is the woman most likely to.

RIGHT In 1988 Nigel Short (left) and Jon Speelman battled to become the first British world semi-finalist.

OVERLEAF Late nineteenth-century glass set, manufactured in Millville, USA.

OVERLEAF, FACING PAGE Selection of eighteenth- and nineteenth-century Muslim pieces.

Kasparov v. Karpov

White: Gary Kasparov;
Black: Anatoly Karpov
Nimzo-Indian Defence, 11th
Game World Championship
Match, Moscow 1985.

1 d4 Nf6 **2** c4 e6 **3** Nc3
Bb4 **4** Nf3 0-0 **5** Bg5 c5
6 e3 cxd4 **7** exd4 h6 **8** Bh4
d5 **9** Rc1 dxc4 **10** Bxc4
Nc6 **11** 0-0 Be7 **12** Re1 b6

13 a3 Bb7 **14** Bg3 Rc8
15 Ba2 Bd6 **16** d5 Nxd5
17 Nxd5 Bxg3 **18** hxg3
exd5 **19** Bxd5 Qf6 **20** Qa4
Rfd8 **21** Rcd1 Rd7 **22** Qg4

Rcd8 **23** Qxd7 Rxd7
24 Re8+ Kh7 **25** Be4+
Black resigns, for if **25** ... g6
26 Rxd7 Ba6 **27** Bxc6 Qxc6
28 Rxf7 is mate.

Position after **8** ... d5

Position after **15** ... Bd6

Position after **22** ... Rcd8

Position after **25** ... Be4+

B E L O W Perpetual rivals – Gary Kasparov (right) and Anatoly Karpov in 1982. R I G H T Kasparov jubilant after retaining his title against Karpov in Seville in 1987.

away by the war, so fierce opposition to Tarrasch as the supreme teacher, was on the horizon.

Aron Nimzowitsch (7 November 1886–16 March 1935) was the leading hypermodern grandmaster. Tarrasch had pushed classicism to its limits. But this antiseptic view of chess failed to take account of a new irrationalism, a psychological interpretation. This turned the old truths on their head, revealing hidden mysteries which injected fresh fight into a game which was becoming excessively technical.

Aron Nimzowitsch was born in Riga, but later emigrated to Denmark. His most important and influential work, *My System*, was a direct challenge to Tarrasch. The hypermodern school held (amongst other things) that control of the centre did not necessarily derive from occupation by pawns. Nimzowitsch also advocated the concept of 'Heroic Defence'. By this he meant the deliberate selection of difficult positions, in order to drag the opponent onto a precipice, where draws would be unlikely and one player would tumble to his doom. This cast of thinking, with its messy loose ends and its appeal to raw struggle, must have been anathema to Tarrasch. In fact, though, the process whereby apparently incontrovertible certainties were being challenged in chess was identical to a similar process at work in other branches of contemporary intellectual activity. It could be seen, for example, in the music of that time, the wild rhythms of Stravinsky's *Sacre du Printemps*, in Dada and Surrealism or with the seemingly impenetrable novels of Franz Kafka.

That Nimzowitsch's theories were successful can be deduced from his colossal tournament results, such as first prize in the tournament at Dresden 1926, ahead of Alekhine, and again, at Carlsbad 1929, ahead of Capablanca. Since the mid-1920s, *My System* has, in fact, been regarded as the essential book to read on chess strategy.

Nimzowitsch's vision may have been revolutionary, but it still retained static elements. His creed, expressed in *My System*, could be summarized as: 'first restrain, then blockade, finally destroy.' In some ways Nimzowitsch concentrated on draining the opponent's dynamism, rather than increasing his own. At other times, he achieved results by luring his opponents into attacks on himself, which he would beat back with relish. Nevertheless, the true spark of dynamism somehow eluded him. He could never, for example, match the impressive blitzkrieg style of an Alekhine.

If this dynamism, so vital to modern chess, and visible in the games, for example, of Tal, Fischer and Kasparov, is anywhere encapsulated, it must be in Bronstein's massive book, *The Chess Struggle in Practice*. David Bronstein (19 February 1924–) came as close as is possible to winning the World Championship. In 1951 he tied a match with Botvinnik in Moscow, but this meant that the defending champion (Botvinnik) retained the title. Two years later, in the Candidates' Tournament of Zürich 1953, Bronstein made a renewed effort to qualify for a title match. He failed, but he failed magnificently. His book on the Candidates' Tournament (*The Chess Struggle in Practice*) has become a modern classic. In it, Bronstein guides the reader through no fewer than 210 games by top grandmasters, explaining in minute detail the thinking behind such dynamic openings as the King's Indian Defence, the new variations of the Nimzo-Indian, the Volga Gambit in the Benoni and many others. This book has become, for so many subsequent generations of grandmasters, the Bible of modern chess.

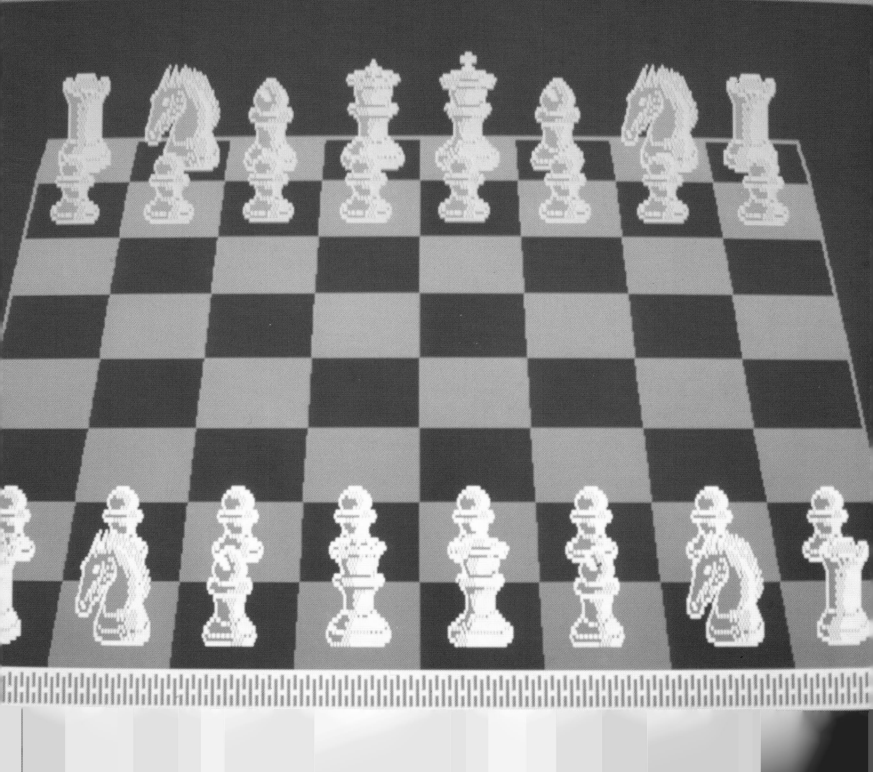

'THE average length of a game between evenly matched opponents of average strength is 40–45 complete moves, but it may be a modest 25. Thus in order to decide on the perfect opening move a computer would have to calculate at least 25 moves ahead. Calculating 25 moves ahead would mean that the machine would have to generate a total number of moves in the order of 10 to the power of 75 (1 and 75 zeros). Even if the computer could operate at the rate of a million moves every second, it would take 10 to the power of 69 seconds to complete the calculation. Ever since our planetary system came into being, some 4.5 billion years ago, no more than 10 to the power of 18 seconds have elapsed.' (Arthur Koestler).

The first attempt at creating a chess-playing machine had more to do with magic and illusion than with science. The earliest chess-playing machine was 'The Turk'. This was a complex automaton, exhibited by the Hungarian engineer and inventor, Baron Wolfgang von Kempelen at the Royal Palace in Vienna in 1769. Von Kempelen was the Counsellor on Mechanics to the Austrian imperial court and he was renowned for his ingenious mechanical devices.

'The Turk' was, in essence, a chest approximately 1.25 metres long, half a metre wide and one metre high. On the top of the chest was a chessboard and behind this sat a lifesize mechanical figure dressed as a turbanned Turk. The baron claimed (could he have been the forerunner of Baron Munchausen?) that the mechanical 'Turk' could play chess. With elaborate ceremony, he would wind up the device and invite members of his audience to challenge the automaton. Clanking into motion the clockwork Turk would pick up a piece with its left hand and slowly and deliberately move it to a new square. At the beginning and end of each exhibition von Kempelen would allow his audience to inspect the mechanism, but nobody could discover its secret. 'The Turk' was, in fact, an elaborate hoax. A human operator was concealed in an internal compartment. The operator – the guest in the machine – was, naturally, a strong, if diminutive, chess player. Hence 'The Turk' won the majority of games against its Austrian courtier opponents. The machine was unfortunately, destroyed by fire in an American museum during the nineteenth century, long after its secret had been revealed.

It was not until the late nineteenth century that the first genuine chess-playing machine was developed. The Spanish scientist Torre y Quevedo invented a mechanism which was able to play the ending of king and rook against a lone king. The machine could only play with the extra rook but, given that, it could always force checkmate. This was a remarkable advance on von Kempelen's legerdemain. Quevedo's machine still functions today and it is on show in Madrid's Polytechnic Museum.

Progress on automated chess stagnated until the 1940s when Alan Turing, a member of the Bletchley Decoding Unit during World War II, and the American scientist, Claude Shannon, outlined some ideas on how to program computers to play the game. Doubtless, Turing's experience of breaking German codes came in useful here. His efforts were commemorated in the play *Breaking the Code* which ran for several years on the London stage in the mid-1980s. This play also drew attention to his deep interest in chess.

By 1958, the first computer chess program was fully operational and within 12 years a sufficient variety of programs existed for a chess tournament to be held in which all the contestants were computer programs. Interest in this fascinating new area of chess investigation suddenly exploded. In 1974 at Stockholm in Sweden the first World Computer Chess Championship attracted no fewer than 13 entries. The winner was the Soviet pro-

Suspicion of the potential of artificial intelligence for making a fool of its creator underlies many human interactions with computers. Commercial computers are often programmed to ask embarrassing questions. They may not snigger, but do commonly ask, 'Do you have a rating?'

116

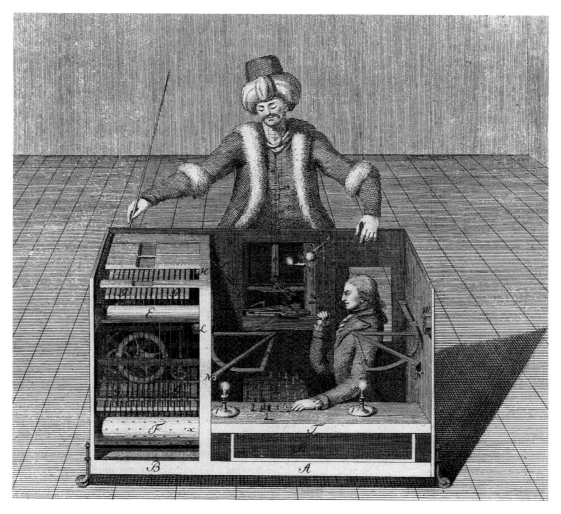

EVERY TIME MAKE A MOVE — IT SNIGGERS!

gram Kaissa, produced by the Moscow Institute of Control Science. This Soviet triumph was short-lived. The championship has now become a regular event, but since 1974 every winner has been a program written in the USA.

In 1977 a remarkable event occurred: a small chess-playing computer appeared on the market. Its level of play was execrable, but the amazing thing was that such a concoction of metal and plastic could play recognizable chess at all. Since those early days, a symbiotic relationship between programmers of the big university mainframes and those working on the production of chess computers for the marketplace, has led to an astonishing increase in the strength and variety of the commercial products. Each new advance in the academic field is mirrored by an increase in strength of the home micros. Commercial chess computers now compete regularly in open tournaments, and have notched up some notable scalps, including those of some international class players.

Since the beginning of the computer age man has lived with the fear that he is, perhaps, not the most intelligent being on earth. The chess computer programmers are determined to lend this fear a proper grounding in science. Early attempts at programming were directed towards the 'brute force' approach. The computer searched almost all variations to the same depth, examining millions of positions in its quest for the best move. Human

117

Man v. Machine

White: Bent Larsen;
Black: Deep Thought
English Opening, Long
Beach, California 1988.

1 c4 e5 **2** g3 Nf6 **3** Bg2 c6
4 Nf3 e4 **5** Nd4 d5 **6** cxd5
Qxd5 **7** Nc2 Qh5 **8** h4 Bf5
9 Ne3 Bc5 **10** Qb3 b6
11 Qa4 0-0 **12** Nc3 b5
13 Qc2 Bxe3 **14** dxe3 Re8
15 a4 b4 **16** Nb1 Nbd7

17 Nd2 Re6 **18** b3 Rd8
19 Bb2 Bg6 **20** Nc4 Nd5
21 0-0-0 N7f6 **22** Bh3 Bf5
23 Bxf5 Qxf5 **24** f3 h5
25 Bd4 Rd7 **26** Kb2 Rc7
27 g4 hxg4 **28** Rhg1 c5
29 fxg4 Nxg4 **30** Bxg7 Rg6

31 Qd2 Rd7 **32** Rxg4 Rxg4
33 Ne5 Nxe3 **34** Qxd7
Nxd1+ **35** Qxd1 Rg3
36 Qd6 Kxg7 **37** Nd7 Re3
38 Qh2 Kh7 **39** Nf8+ Kh8
40 h5 Qd5 **41** Ng6+ fxg6
42 hxg6 dis+ Kg7 **43** Qh7+
Kf6 White resigns.

Position after **11** . . . 0-0

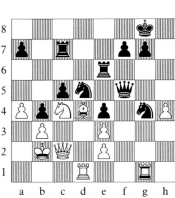

Position after **22** . . . Bf5

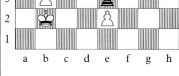

Position after **29** . . . Nxg4

Position after **37** . . . Re3

Modern portable chess computers are ideal travelling companions on long journeys. The plastic computer set seen here measures just 18 square inches and can be slipped into a pocket.

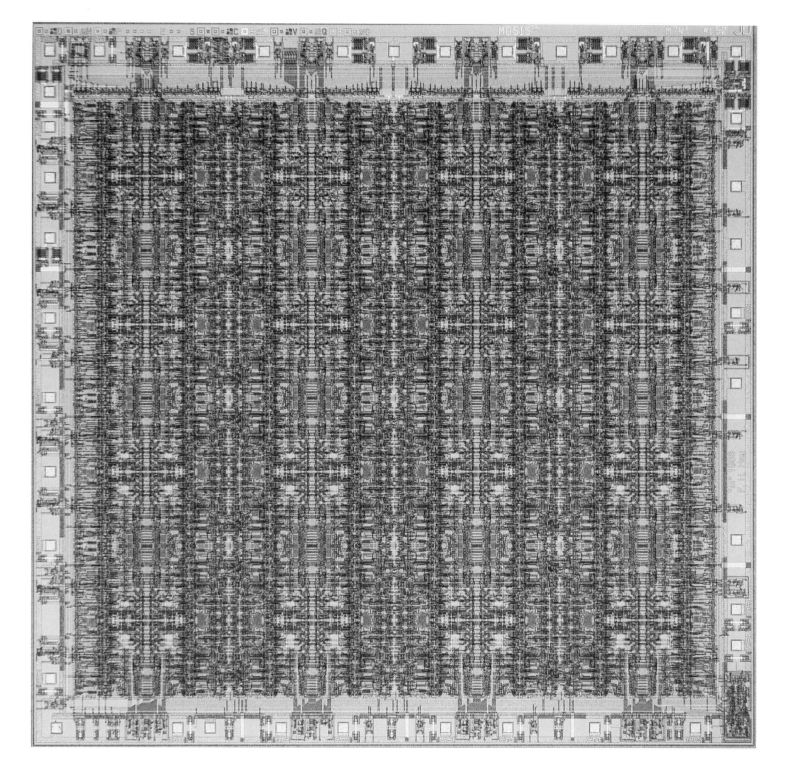

*Microchip from the brain of
Deep Thought, the world's
most successful chess computer.
In October 1989 Gary*

*Kasparov struck a blow for
humankind by beating the
machine 2-0.*

players, however, do not play chess in this way, they tend to consider a narrow range of moves, concentrating on analysis of the most promising ones. Experience tells the human chess master that in most positions no more than two or three moves will be playable. In 1968 David Levy, who was to become an international chess master and later President of the International Computer Chess Association, wagered that no computer program would be able to beat him within a decade. In 1978 Levy won his bet, defeating the then world computer champion CHESS 4.7 in a match in Toronto. Since then, greater progress has been made by the metal minds.

The main weaknesses of chess programs can be traced to their inability to plan ahead and to their relatively feeble grasp of strategic concepts. In the tactical domain, though, computers are extremely adept and can examine certain forcing variations to a vastly greater depth than human beings ever could. Thus it follows that computers can handle certain complex, if rare endgames, with total accuracy. This embraces the endgame, notoriously difficult for a human, of two bishops versus knight, and the endgame of king and queen against king and rook. US programmer Ken Thompson has demonstrated that there are four million separate possible positions in the latter endgame and his program has proved beyond doubt that no winning line should take more than 31 moves. Thompson's computer, therefore, plays this endgame with vastly greater skill than most human grandmasters.

The ultimate aim for computer chess experts lies in the construction of a program that can beat the human world champion. Professor Hans Berliner, head of the Deep Thought Chess Computer Project at Carnegie-Mellon Computer Science Department, University of Pittsburgh, warns that in about three years' time his team will produce a computer able to defeat Gary Kasparov. Kasparov himself is less convinced. Computer experts believe that the writing of chess programs can help us to learn about the ways in which human

Chess-playing programs are very popular for personal computers. The program here is competing in the first computer Olympics, held in London in the summer of 1989.

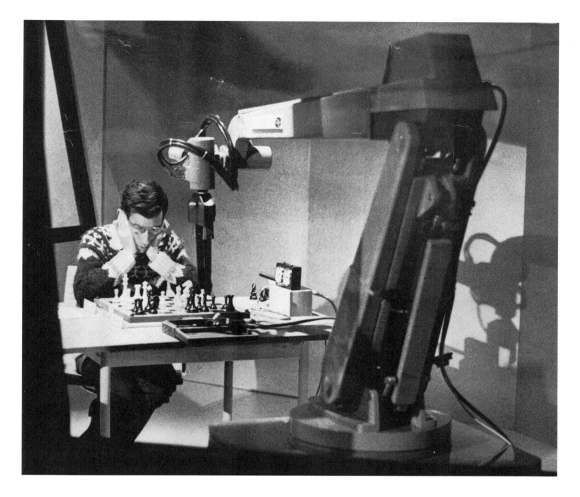

David Levy, President of the International Chess Association, under threat from a chess-playing robot. In December 1989 Deep Thought challenged Levy in the hope of re-establishing its reputation after its disaster against Kasparov.

beings think. A further by-product is the insight which can be gained into the development of programming techniques for use in other spheres, such as military research. Indeed, the Deep Thought Project has been partially funded by the Pentagon's Defense Advanced Research Project Agency (DARPA).

The most recent developments on the chess front do point to computers being likely challengers for top honours, even against human grandmasters, in the future. Towards the end of 1988 Deep Thought, whose main programmer is the Taiwanese graduate student, Feng-Hsiung Hsu, tied for first place at the Long Beach, California, tournament with the former British grandmaster, Tony Miles. Deep Thought left in its wake the former world champion, Mikhail Tal, and en route the machine inflicted defeat on three times World Championship semi-finalist, Bent Larsen.

Deep Thought uses a modified version of the brute force approach. There are more possible chess games than there are atoms in the known universe. Deep Thought, therefore, limits its search to a depth of 10 moves in most variations. If it did not do this, the machine, searching more or less ad infinitum, would take more than seven and a half million years just to play its first move. Nevertheless, Deep Thought, even in its restricted mode, examines an incredible 1,500,000 positions every second. Since this capacity is millions of times quicker than even the strongest human chess players, Gary Kasparov may well have to watch out.

OVERLEAF Wichmann chess set.

121

CHRONOLOGY

BC

3000   Senet, primitive board game, played in ancient Egypt.

1500   Gaming pieces and dice closely resembling modern chess pieces in use in Lothal and Harappan civilization, India.

400   Petteia, a battle game of reason and strategy, played in classical Greece.

330   Around this time, Alexander invades Asia, establishes Hellenic colonies.

300   From this time on Greek games of reason encounter Indian dice games of chance.

AD

200   Gaming pieces of the Roman imperial period from Venafro, Italy, closely resembling 'Islamic' chessmen.

600   Chaturanga, the precursor of chatrang, shatranj and chess, recorded in India.

600   The first ever reference to chess (chatrang) in literature in a Persian romance.

651   Arabic conquest of Persia completed, shatranj popular, spreads west toward Europe.

712   Seville conquered by Arabs. Moorish invaders bring chess to Iberian peninsula.

786   Reign of Harun Ar-Rashid, Caliph of Islam. Shatranj golden age begins.

946   Death of As-Suli, the strongest player of shatranj in the Baghdad caliphate.

1000   Chess popular throughout Europe (still the old, slow version).

1100   Chess mentioned in the Carolingian epic *The Song of Roland*.

1148   *Alexiad* of Anna Comnena mentions Byzantine Emperor Alexius Comnenus playing chess.

1250   *Mabinogion*, Welsh epic, attains written form: King Arthur plays 'Gwyddbyll' against Owein.

1283   Alfonso the Wise (King of Castile and Leon) orders illustrated chess manuscript.

1300   Chess 'morality' (*Liber de Moribus* ...) written by Dominican friar, Jacobus de Cessolis.

1450   'Civis Bononiae', collection of tricky problems, incorporated in Florentine manuscript.

1467   Francesco Colonna's Italian *Hypnerotomachia Poliphili* describes chess ballet.

1474   Caxton publishes *The Game and Playe of the Chesse*.

1475   Around this time, new chess takes hold: queen and bishop assume modern powers.

1495   Vicent publishes first practical book on new chess in Valencia (all copies now lost).

1497   Lucena publishes in Salamanca oldest surviving book on practical play in new chess.

1512   Damiano (Portuguese) publishes at Rome first chess book to appear in Italy.

1513   Vida writes chess poem *Scacchia Ludus* (Basle 1525).

1561   Spanish priest, Ruy Lopez, publishes comprehensive chess book.

1594   Polerio, champion of Rome, dedicates chess treatise to Duke of Sora.

1597   Gianutio publishes first book of late sixteenth-century Italian school at Turin.

1600   Castling established as a single move, but still many regional variations.

1604   Salvio publishes in Naples first work to detail advances made by sixteenth-century Italians.

1613   Chess on stage in Shakespeare's *The Tempest* (Miranda playing Ferdinand).

1616   Polymath 'Selenus' (the Duke of Brunswick-Lüneburg) writes first German chess book.

1617   Sicilian priest, Carrera, publishes *Il Gioco degli Scacchi*, book of chess instruction.

1624   *A Game At Chess* by Middleton at the Globe Theatre. Play suppressed after nine days by James I.

1634   Death of Greco in the West Indies, the strongest player of his day.

1747   Philidor defeats Stamma in match at Slaughter's Coffee House in London.

1749   Philidor publishes his *Analyse des échecs*, first book to explain importance of pawns.

1769   Von Kempelen's 'Turk', the automaton chess player, exhibited in Vienna.

1813   First ever chess column published in the *Liverpool Mercury*.

1831   Isle of Lewis chessmen discovered (twelfth-century Scandinavian), oldest complete set.

1834   Labourdonnais wins overall in series of six matches against McDonnell, London.

1836   *Le Palamede*, the first chess magazine, published in Paris.

1843   English champion, Howard Staunton, defeats Saint Amant in great match in Paris.

1849 Staunton endorses Nathaniel Cooke's chess pieces (knight inspired by Elgin Marbles).

1851 Immortal game between Anderssen and Kieseritsky, played at Simpson's in London. First ever international chess tournament, in London. Anderssen (Germany) wins.

1857 Paul Morphy wins first US tournament, New York.

1858 Morphy travels to Europe and defeats best masters, including Anderssen.

1859 Morphy gives up serious chess.

1872 Lewis Carroll writes *Through the Looking Glass and What Alice Found There*.

1884 Morphy, a paranoid recluse, dies of apoplexy in his bath at New Orleans.

1886 Steinitz defeats Zukertort in America in first official World Championship match.

1894 Lasker beats Steinitz, Montreal/New York/Philadelphia, becomes second world champion.

1914 Lasker wins great tournament at St Petersburg ahead of Capablanca, Alekhine, Tarrasch.

1921 Capablanca defeats Lasker in Havana and becomes world champion.

1924 FIDE, the World Chess Federation, founded in Paris.

1925 Nimzowitsch publishes *My System*, possibly most influential chess book ever written.

1927 First Chess Olympics, held in London (Hungary Gold, Denmark Silver, England Bronze). Alekhine becomes world champion, defeating Capablanca in marathon, at Buenos Aires.

1935 Dutch Grandmaster Euwe beats Alekhine to become world champion.

1937 Alekhine beats Euwe in revenge match, first player ever to regain world title.

1938 AVRO Tournament in Holland, second strongest in history. Keres and Fine tie first.

1946 World champion Alekhine dies in Portugal. FIDE takes control of championship.

1948 Botvinnik first Soviet world champion, strongest ever tournament (The Hague/Moscow).

1957 Smyslov beats Botvinnik to become world champion, loses title back next year.

1960 Tal beats Botvinnik in Moscow, becomes world champion, but loses title back next year.

1963 Petrosian beats Botvinnik, becomes world champion. Revenge

match abolished.

1969 Spassky beats Petrosian in Moscow to become world champion.

1970 FIDE introduces Elo Rating List to assess players' strengths. Soviet team defeats Rest of World at Belgrade. Dr Max Euwe (former world champion) elected President of FIDE.

1972 Fischer beats Spassky in Reykjavik, becomes world champion, but never plays again.

1974 First World Computer Championship, held in Stockholm.

1975 Fischer defaults his world title without play to the young Russian, Anatoly Karpov.

1977 FIDE reinstates revenge match clause for a defeated world champion.

1978 Karpov defends his world title in the Philippines against the Soviet defector, Korchnoi. Icelandic Grandmaster Fridrik Olafsson elected FIDE President in Buenos Aires.

1982 At the Lucerne Congress of the World Chess Federation, Campomanes elected President.

1984 Soviet team beats Rest of World team in London. Soviet Union wins Olympic Gold and England takes the Silver.

1985 (15 February) FIDE President Campomanes halts World Championship match in Moscow. (November) Kasparov beats Karpov in new match in Moscow to become youngest champion.

1986 Tim Rice/Abba, *Chess*, on the London stage. Kasparov retains world title against Karpov in London/Leningrad revenge match. FIDE abolishes once again right to revenge match for defeated world champion. Grandmaster Association founded in Dubai, with Kasparov as President. Soviet Union win Gold at Olympics in Dubai, England Silver, USA Bronze.

1987 Kasparov draws match with Karpov in Seville and retains world title.

1988 Joel Lautier, France, wins Junior World Championship in Australia. Deep Thought computer beats Bent Larsen in California (first machine win against grandmaster). 12-year-old Judit Polgar (Hungary) becomes youngest ever International Master. Soviet Union wins Olympic Gold in Thessaloniki, England Silver, Holland Bronze.

1988/89 Inauguration of Grandmaster Association World Cup (£1.2 million prize fund).

1989 Deep Thought wins World Computer Championship, Edmonton, Canada. First Computer Olympics, in London; chess and Chinese chess programs play. Deep Thought team predicts they will beat human world champion in 4–5 years.

BIBLIOGRAPHY

Austin, 'Greek Board Games' *Antiquity* 1940
Bijl, Christian, *Die Gesammelten Partien von Robert J Fischer* The Hague, 1986
Bronstein, David, *The Chess Struggle in Practice* London 1980
Davies, Vivian, *Egyptian Hieroglyphs* London 1987
Divinsky, Nathan & Keene, Raymond, *Warriors of the Mind* London 1989
Eales, Richard, *Chess, The History of a Game* London 1985
Golombek, Harry, *Encyclopaedia of Chess* London 1978
Golombek, Harry, *Réti's Best Games of Chess* London 1954
Golombek, Harry, & Koestler, Arthur, *Fischer v Spassky* London 1973
Hooper, David & Whyld, Ken, *The Oxford Companion to Chess* Oxford 1984
Ivkov, Borislav, *Sahovske Lepotice* Belgrade 1973
Karpov, Anatoly, *V Dalekom Bagio* Moscow 1978

Kasparov, Gary & Trelford, Donald, *Child of Change* London 1987
Keene, Raymond *The Chess Combination from Philidor to Karpov* London 1977
Keene, Raymond & Goodman, David, *Manoeuvres in Moscow* London 1985
Lawson, Dominic, 'Playing to Win – The Pentagon's War Moves' *The Spectator*, 28 January 1989
Levy, David & O'Connell, Kevin, *Oxford Encyclopaedia of Chess Games 1485–1866* Oxford 1981
Murray, H.J.R., *A History of Chess* Oxford 1913
Nimzowitsch, Aron, *My System* London 1929
Panov, V., *Capablanca* Moscow 1970
Tarrasch, Siegbert, *Dreihundert Schachpartien* Gouda 1925
Zarate, Augustin de, *The Discovery and Conquest of Peru* London 1968

PICTURE ACKNOWLEDGEMENTS

The Publishers would like to thank Lark Gilmer and Derrick Witty for the special photography they undertook for this book, and particularly Gareth Williams for all his assistance in the picture research and for so generously allowing access to his private chess collection. They also wish to thank the following:

Lothar Alt: 121
Asprey Plc: 54, 55
Bargello, Florence: 27, 35
Simon Bell: 118
Bridgeman Art Library: 39
The British Museum: 12, 13, 14–15, 16–17, 24, 56
© Peter Brooke/*Spectator*: 109b
Mrs Capablanca Clarke: 72
© Peter Clarke: 116–17
Cleveland Public Library Ohio, Special Collections, White Collection of Chess: 28
Feng Hsiung Hsu, Carnegie Mellon University, Pittsburgh: 119
Germanisches Museum, Nuremberg: 46–7
Giraudon, Paris: 16 top, 98
Haags Gemeentemuseum, The Hague: 100–01
© 1990 M. C. Escher Heirs/Cordon Art – Baarn – Holland: 100–01
Mr David Hafler, Philadelphia: 30–1, 90–1, 94–5
Paper chess set for Museum of Modern Art, New York, © 1988 Peter Hewitt: 107
Michael Holford: 18, 21, 26
Mark Huba: 109 top r.
© Bill Jacklin/Marlborough Fine Art Gallery: 99
John Jaques and Son Ltd: 50
David King: 89 top r.
Koninklijke Bibliotheek, The Hague: half-title-page, 117
Lark Gilmer: 2–3, 6–7, 10, 11, 23, 31, 43, 49, 51, 63, 70–1, 87, 107, 110, 111, 115

The Late David Lawson Collection: 66, 67, 69
Michael Mark Collection: 34, 45b, 52–3, 57, 60, 61, 63
Magnum Photos Ltd: 67, 128
Melgar Photographers, California: 119
Metropolitan Museum of Art, New York, Bequest of Maitland and Maitland F. Griggs 1943 Maitland F Griggs Collection (43.98.8): 38
© Jeremy Morgan/*Spectator*: 109
Collection, The Museum of Modern Art, New York: 101 top r. – Etching printed in black $7^2/8'' \times 6^1/4''$, gift of Ludwig Charell © ADAGP, Paris/DACS London 1990; 102 – bronze (cast 1954) $38^1/2 \times 18^3/4'' \times 20^1/2''$, gift of D. and J. de Menil. © DACS 1990
Novosti Press: 108, 112
Oxford Mobius, Programme, Oxford Chess © 1988: 115
Philadelphia Museum of Art: 103, Oil on canvas, $39^3/4 \times 39^3/4$ The Louise and Walter Arensberg Collection. © ADAGP, Paris/DACS, London 1990
Pierpont Morgan Library, New York: 22
Pictorial Parade: 96, 97
Reuters/Bettman Newsphotos: 113
© Rodchenko Estate/Museum of Modern Art, Oxford: 88–9
Savoy Hotel Group: 65
Scala, Florence: 27, 35
Society for Cultural Relations with the USSR: 92, 93, 97l, 97r
Staatliche Graphische Sammlung, Munich: 33
The Times Newspapers Limited: 104 © Richard Wilson; 109 top l., 120
Victoria and Albert Museum: 9, 18, 19, 25
Christian Wichmann: 122–123
Gareth Williams Collection: 2, 3, 6, 7, 10, 11, 13, 23, 31, 36, 37, 42, 43, 48, 49, 51, 52–3, 58–9, 60, 66, 69, 70, 71, 72–3, 76, 77, 79, 83, 85, 87, 88, 105, 110, 111, 116–17
Derrick Witty: 13, 29, 34, 36, 37, 45, 48, 49, 52, 52–3, 53, 57, 58–9, 60, 60–1, 72, 73, 76–7, 76, 79, 83, 85, 88, 105, 116–17

INDEX

Numbers in *italics* refer to illustrations.

Adams, Michael 106, *109*
Al-Adli 16
Alekhine, Alexander 41, 67, 73, 76, 84–6, 100
Alexander the Great 12, 14, 17
Alexius Comnenus, Emperor 8, 12
Al-Lajlaj 16
Aristotle 14
Anderssen, Adolph 40, 48, 62, 64, 68, 81
Ar-Razi 16
As-Suli 16, 21, 22
AVRO (1938) 67

backgammon 10
Baghdad: shatranj in 16, 21, 22
Barbier, J.: *The Famous Game of Chesse-play* 29
Barcelona: World Cup at 32
Berliner, Hans 120
Bernstein, Ossipp 83
bishop 8, 17; moves of 8, 29; *see also* elephant
Boi, Paolo 37
Bonnerjee, Moheshunder 108
Botvinnik, Mikhail 40, 41, 67, 73, 76–8, 86, 88–9, 92, 93, 108, *97*, *100*
Botvinnik Rule 76
Boy's Own Paper 76
Bray, Jan de 100, *half-title*
Bronstein, David 108, 114; *The Chess Struggle in Practice* 114
Bugdanov, A. *89*

Campomanes, Florencio 79
Capablanca, José 40, 41, 67, 69, 73, 82, 83–4, 108, *72*; game by 72
Caro, Horatio 41
Caro-Kann Defence 41
Carrera, Pietro: *Il Gioco degli Scacchi* 40
castle *see* rook
castling 8, 24, 28
Caxton, William: *Game and Playe of the Chesse 36*, 37
chaturanga 14–15
chess: Arabic *see* shatranj: in art 100; appeal of 10; blitz 93; in cartoons *83, 84–5, 104, 105, 116–17*; on cigarette cards *74–5, 77*; computers in 68, 105, 116–21, *118, 119, 120*; games comparable with *see* go, shogi; history of 8, 10, 12–22, 24–32, *13*; in journals 81, 76; openings in 40–1, 108; origins of 8, 12, 14, 15; rules of 8–9; in schools 76; simultaneous *58–9*;

spread of, eastwards 8, 16; spread of, westwards 16; symbolism of 22, 100, *22, 24*; as warfare 8, 10, 12, 24–32, *33, 83*; women in *79*
chessboards 9, *18, 35, 54, 55, 65*; computerized *115, 118*
chess clocks 64, *63*
chess pieces *11, 16, 17, 48–9, 87, 111*; 'Bust' *52–3*; Charlemagne *16*; history of 8, 17; Isle of Lewis 22, *26*; names of 17, 20; Staunton 44, *50, 51*; *see also under names of individual pieces*
chess sets 100; for blind *60–1*; Chinese *10, 53, 61*; computerized *118*; French *23, 52–3*; German *46–7*; glass *110*; Indian *title-page, 52, 54*; Jaques *43*; metal *102*; miniature *43*; 'Pepys' *52*; Russian *60, 90–1, 94–5*; for soldiers *61*; travelling *43, 60, 118*; Wichmann *122–3*
chess tournaments 44–62, 64, 68, 104, *67*; *see also* World Championship
China: chess in 16, *10*
Cochrane, John 108
Columbus, Christopher 32, 37
computers *see* chess, computers in
Constantinople: chess played in 8
Cooke, Nathaniel 44, 50
Cratinus 14
Cutri, Leonardo da 37

Daumier, Honoré 100; *Chess Players 98*
DARPA 121
Deep Thought 105, 121, *119*; game by 118; Project 120–1
draughts 10
Duchamp, Marcel 100, 102: *Chess Players* (1909) 100; *The Large Glass* 100; *Portrait of Chess Players* (1911) *103*

Egypt, ancient 12, 13
elephant *27, 31*; forerunner of bishop 8, 17, *18*; moves of 20
Elo ranking system 106
endgames 120
England: chess in 9
English Opening 41
Ernst, Max 100; 'The King Playing with his Queen' *102*
Escher, M.C.: *Metamorphose 100–1*
Euwe, Max 73, 76, 84, 86, *105*; quoted 44

Feng-Hsiung Hsu 121
FIDE 9, 73, 76, 78, 86, 93
Fine, Reuben 67

Fischer, Bobby (Robert) 40, 78, 88, 96, 104, 105, 106, 108, *105*; compared with Morphy 62; game by 105
French Defence 41

'Game of Twenty Squares' 13, *14–15*
Grandmaster Association 78, 79
Georghiu, Florin 66
Girolamo da Cremona: 'The Chess Players' *38*
go 8, 10
Golombek, Harry 41
Gorky, M. *89*
Greco, Gioacchino 40, 42; *Primo Modo di Gioco de Partito 34*; game by 34
Greece, ancient *13*
Gris, Jan 100

'Il Dilettevole Givdizioso Givoco de Scacchi' *28*
India: chess in 8
'Immortal Game' 48, 62, 81
Ivanchuck, Vassily 106

Jacklin, Bill: *The Chess Players 99*
Japan, chess in *see* shogi
Jaques Company 44, 50

Kaissa 116–17
Kandinsky, Vassily 100
Kann, Marcus 41
Karpov, Anatoly 32, 40, 41, 64, 76, 78, 104–6, 108, *112*; game by 112
Kasparov, Gary 32, 40, 41, 64, 76, 78, 79, 86, 92, 104, 106, 108, 119, 120, *112, 113*; game by 112
Kempelen, Baron Wolfgang von 116
Keres, Paul 67, 73, *100*
Kieseritzky, Lionel 48
king 8, *87*; moves of 20, 28
King's Gambit 40, *88*
King's Indian Defence 108
Klee, Paul 100
knight 8, *26, 70–1*; moves of 20, 29
Koestler, Arthur: quoted 116
kubeia 14

Labourdonnais, L.C. de 68
Larsen, Bent 121; game by 118
Lasker, Emanuel 41, 69, 82–3, *69, 73*
Lautier, Joel 106
Leibnitz, G.W. von: quoted 8
Lenin, V.I. *89*
Levy, David, 120, *121*
London: 1851 tournament 44–62; 1883 tournament 64; World Championship (1986) 64 '

Lopez, Ruy 37, 40, 41, 42; *Libro . . . del Juego de Axedrez* 37; opening called after 40, 42
Lucena, Luis Ramirez de 40, 41; *Repeticion de . . . Arte de Axedres* 40
'Ludus Duodecim Scriptorum' 14

Mabinogion 22
McKnight Kauffer, E.: costume design for *Checkmate 101*
Madrid: 1575 match at 37
Mahabharata 14
Man, Cornelis de 100; 'The Chess Players' *39*
Marshall, Frank 73
Master E.S. 24
Mecking, Enrique 66
Mesopotamia 12
Middle Ages, chess in 22, *22, 24, 25*
Miles, Tony 121
Mnemonic des Schachspieles 45
Morphy, Paul 56–7, 62, 64, 68; game by 57
Moscow: 1946 match *93*

New York: 1857 chess congress 56, *57*; first official World Championship (1886) 50, 81; 1924 tournament 82
Nimzo-Indian Defence 108
Nimzowitsch, Aron 41, 83, 84, 108, 114, *73*; *My System* 114

Oxford Mobius: *Oxford Chess 115*

Paulsen, Louis 57, 64, 108
pawn 8, *16*; moves of 8, 20, 24, 29
Petrosian, Tigran 41, 68, 78, 89, 93–6, 108, *96*
petteia 14, *13*
Philidor, François-André Danican 41, 44, 68, *45*; game by 45; *L'Analyse des échecs* 44, 45
Philip II of Spain 37
Pillsbury, Harry Nelson *69*
Plato 14
Polerio, Giulio Cesare 40, 41
Polgar, Judit 40, 106, *109*

queen 8, *6–7, 30*; moves of 24, 28; *see also* vizier
Queen's Gambit 40–1
Quevedo, Torre y 116

Rabrab 16
Renaissance *32*; chess in 24–32, 37
Reshevsky, Samuel 73, *93*
Réti, Richard 41, 83, 108
Réti's Opening 108

Reykjavik: 1972 World
Championship 96, 105, *105*
rook 8, 17; moves of 20, 28
Rodchenko, Alexander *88–9*
Rosenthal, M. *58–9*

Sadler, Matthew 106
Saint Amant, F. de 41, 44
St Petersburg: 1896 tournament *69*;
  1914 tournament 82, *73*
Salvio, Alessandro 40
San Sebastian: 1911 tournament
  83–4
'Selenus' (Duke of Brunswick-
  Lüneburg): *Das Schach- oder
  Königspiel 42*
senet 12, 13, 100, *12*
Seville: 1987 World Championship
  32, 41

Shannon, Claude 116
shatranj 16, 21, *21*; moves of 20;
  openings in 21
shogi 8, 10, 16
Short, Nigel *109*
Sicilian Defence 40
Simpson's-in-the-Strand 62, 81, *65*
Slater, Jim *105*
Smyslov, Vassily 41, 73, 78, 88, 89,
  92, 108, *100*
Soviet Union: chess in 9, 88, *67*, *92*
Spassky, Boris 40, 78, 89, 93, 96,
  105, 108, *105*, *108*; game by 105
Speelman, Jon *109*
Staight, Thomas 48–9
Stamma, Philip 40–1; *The Noble
  Game of Chess 40*
Staunton, Howard 40, 41, 44, 62,
  64, 68, *49*; *The Chess Tournament*

62
Steinitz, Wilhelm 40, 66, 68, 68–9,
  81, 82, *65*, *80*
Szen, Joseph: quoted 62

'Tabula' 14
Tal, Mikhail 40, 78, 88, 89, 92–3,
  108, 121, *97*
Tarrasch, Siegbert 106–14, *80*;
  Dreihundert Schachpartien
  106; *Die Moderne Schachpartie*
  106
Tchigorin, Mikhail 81, *80*
Tenniel, Sir John: illustrations to
  Lewis Carroll *104*
Thompson, Ken 120
Tolstoy, Count Leo *88*
Turing, Alan 116
'Turk, The' 116, *117*

USA: chess in 9

Villon, Jacques: *Chess Board 101*
vizier: forerunner of queen 8; moves
  of 20

Weber, Paul: sketch *85*
World Championship 68, 69–78;
  (1886) 68, 81; (1910) 69, 76;
  (1921) 84; (1927) 76, 84; (1948)
  67, 86, 100; (1966) 93; (1972) 96;
  (1986) 64; (1987) 32
World Chess Federation *see* FIDE
World Computer Chess
  Championship 116–17

Zukertort, Johannes 50, 68, 69, 81,
  108, *65*, *69*, *80*

Index by Jennifer Speake

*Unseen opponent. A game is set up in a corridor of
Attica Prison, New York*